BUDDHIST STORIES

PAUL DAHLKE

TRANSLATED BY

THE BHIKKHU SILACARA

GYAN

Published by

Gyan Publishing House
5, Ansari Road
Daryaganj, New Delhi-110002
Phone: 011-47034999, 9811692060
E-mail: books@gyanbooks.com

Distribution Network
gyanbooks.com
India, USA, Canada, UK, Australia, France

ISBN: 978-81-212-9077-7 (PB)
First Published, 1913

2nd Impression 2023

Printed at: Gyan Press, Delhi.

BUDDHIST STORIES

AUTHOR: PAUL DAHLKE

BUDDHIST STORIES

BUDDHIST STORIES

BY

PAUL DAHLKE

AUTHOR OF "BUDDHIST ESSAYS," "BUDDHISM AND SCIENCE," ETC.

TRANSLATED BY

THE BHIKKHU SĪLACĀRA.

LONDON:

KEGAN PAUL, TRENCH, TRÜBNER & CO., LTD.

BROADWAY HOUSE, 68-74, CARTER LANE, E.C.

1913

BUDDHIST STORIES

DEATH AND LIFE

IN a certain place, not far from Benares, there lived a man, by name Gautama, who, after having experienced something of life, resolved to leave all behind him, and with one or two others to depart from his native place and travel far away.

So, along with these others, he forsook his village, and took nothing with him but a staff and a calabash, and on his body a red robe.

Now when they came to the cross-roads, his companions went straight on. But Gautama thought, "Why should I go straight on? I will turn to the left." The others, however, called to him, "This is where the way lies, Friend Gautama!" But he answered, "My way lies this way," whereupon the others considered, "Leave him alone. What is it to us? He is a fool!"

But now, as Gautama went on alone, he soon found himself in a place where he had never before been. "How is this?" he asked himself. "I am well acquainted with this neighbourhood all around, and yet I never saw this place before." Indeed, it seemed to him as if the sun shone here with another light than it did elsewhere. But he kept stepping boldly on, always towards the east.

As evening approached, he came to a vast desert that spread all round him like a smooth cloth, and before him, like some monstrous thing, lay always his shadow.

Now when Gautama saw the vast desert and the long shadow before him, he thought, "What is this life to me if I do not prevail over death? The lust of money have I overcome. The lust of honour have I overcome. The love of woman have I overcome. But what is all this to me if I do not also vanquish death?"

Thoughtfully and with lowered eyes he went further on.

When next he lifted up his eyes, he saw

before him a lovely little wood, and in it a hut, in front of which in the evening calm sat a grey old man.

Gautama greeted him respectfully. He thought, "I will ask this grey old man. Mayhap he knows how one may vanquish death."

So he went up to him, and, sitting down respectfully by his side, he began—

"Does the venerable one happen to know how one may vanquish death?"

The old man smiled.

"Hast thou yet overcome the lust of gold?" he asked.

"Yes," answered Gautama.

"Hast thou yet overcome the lust of fame?"

"Yes," answered Gautama.

"Hast thou yet overcome the love of woman?"

"Yes," answered Gautama.

"Through what hast thou vanquished the lust of gold?"

"Through doubt."

"Through what hast then vanquished the lust of fame?"

"Through doubt."

"Through what hast thou vanquished the love of woman?"

"Through doubt."

"Tell me," said the old man.

Then this Gautama began to tell—

"Long time I lived in that place not far from Benares, and earned my bread by trafficking. Then one day it happed that all unforeseen I made a great gain. When I saw all the money in a heap together, greed laid hold of me. I began to add to my store penny by penny. When the amount became so great that I could not any longer well keep it by me for fear of thieves, I entrusted it to a brother trader. But now that I possessed money, I lived more miserably than ever. My only joy was the increase of my treasure; my only sorrow that I might some day lose what I had gathered together. But this was the thing most wretched about this wretched condition—I was so entirely taken up with my greed that I had not the faintest notion of its wretchedness. My constant care and anxiety seemed to me to be so natural that I never once thought of asking myself, 'Must this be?'

"One day the man I trusted went bankrupt. My whole fortune was gone. Groaning and rending my hair, I lay in my lodging. Then there came a religious mendicant to my door and begged an alms. I screamed out at him with all my might, 'I have lost my all, and yet you require an alms.'

"Thereupon he silently took his alms-bowl and shook half of its contents into my vessel.

"I said, 'Of what use is that to me?' He said, 'To satisfy your hunger. What more do you wish?'

"I replied, 'I have whereof to eat and to drink without this, but my fortune is gone, all my hoardings.'

"The beggar turned to go. Doing so, he said, 'O thou fool, if thou knewest how sweet is the poverty of those that understand.'

"When he had departed I looked at the rice in my vessel. I became thoughtful. 'This man,' I reflected, 'lives from hand to mouth, and yet he gives away the half of that which he has begged.' But when any one begins to reflect upon his misfortune, already it has lost its bitterest taste; for all lamentation arises from lack of reflection.

"A doubt awoke in me as to whether my previous manner of life had been the right one. Already half comforted, I fell asleep. On the very next day I was thinking quite otherwise of my misfortune. 'What does it matter to you,' I said to myself, 'whether or not you live with the consciousness that such and such a purse of money lies deposited with such and such a merchant? You would just as little have touched any of it as if it had belonged to another; you would have starved yourself to death first. Have you not hitherto lived like one who has placed the most vulnerable part of his body just where it can be got at by every one? Have you not been like a ship in a storm that trails its cargo, tied to a rope, behind it through the waves? Are you not living now just as you were before? Nay, will you not now live more richly and more at peace than ever you did before?'

"It was not very long before I had made such progress in this new way of thinking, that I was earnestly convinced that I had secured a lifelong advantage through the loss of my money.

"With this newly-acquired knowledge I ought well to have been able to lead a quiet and rational life, a life of outward as well as inward equipoise. But further doubts began to torment me. 'Do I now stand sufficiently secure for life, now that I have lost my fortune and carry on this trade? May not this business also some day go to ruin, and shall I not then once more experience a similar, nay, perhaps a greater grief? Were it not better that I take my place of my own free will upon the lowest step, where I can no longer lose anything, simply because I have no more to lose?'

"Thus night and day was I tortured by doubts and fears, like a man unable to confine himself to the happy mean. At last I resolved to give up all and to spend my life in the penance-groves as a religious mendicant.

"Since my mind was in a state of strain when I entered upon this mode of life, I threw myself with ardour into the study of the Vedas * and the practice of mortifications. From the words of another ascetic I one day perceived that I was beginning to attract attention by my strict manner of life. Immediately my ardour redoubled, and soon I was the shining light of this religious company. To me alone was the honour permitted of wearing an iron girdle round my body, to signify that I might burst if my wisdom and intellectual bulk should increase much further.

"Then one day there came to us an alien priest out of the East. He had a reputation for the profoundest learning. A tournament of knowledge was arranged between us, like those contests which men are wont to have between fighting-cocks. Through one question about the seat of the highest Brahman † I involved myself in contradictions. I had a mind to extricate myself by means

* The primitive Hindu Scriptures.
† The first deity in the Hindu triad.

of an untruth. But when my opponent said to me, 'I see a spirit over you with drawn sword, who will cleave your head in twain if you speak falsehood,' I yielded and owned myself vanquished.

"And so my reputation was gone for ever, and in addition I had the consciousness of having been minded to tell a lie in order to save this reputation, which is the worst thing of all for one who strives after purity.

"'Hither then has thy lust of fame brought thee,' I thought, as, dejected and despairing, I sat before the door of my cell. The sweat of the effort and the excitement of the tourney still stood undried upon my brow.

"It happened that a fan lay near me, though I could not say how it came to be there. I took it up mechanically and began to fan myself. As the cooling air passed over my face, the thought came to me—

"'What is this now? When this fan is moved backwards and forwards, a wind arises. May not the great wind that blows over the four quarters of the world arise in a similar fashion? We say, "That is

Indra's * doing, that is Varuna's † doing;" but may it not also be merely the effect of a cause like this tiny breeze here blowing on my face? May not that Gautama be right who call himself the Buddha, and has begun at Benares to turn the wheel of the Law, when he says that there is nothing in the universe save that which, as effect, follows upon cause? And so, gone are all the gods!'

"'Honestly, how do I know that there is something supreme which leads this entire universe along its own chosen path? It may be so; it may not be so. Who can ever prove it one way or another? Oh, if we would only cease from our conjecturings upon the highest things! If we would only seek after what is certain in ourselves! Whether there are gods or not might keep us arguing for a whole year of Brahmā. Lies, however, still remain lies; evil dispositions of the heart still remain evil dispositions of the heart, whether with gods or without them. Verily we must lay hold there where we can hold.'

* The king of heaven.

† The god of rain, clouds and ocean.

"After such a form of doubt as this had laid hold of me, I thought I understood the utter pitiableness of this lust of fame. 'The two of us,' I said to myself, 'have been striving over a thing about which we neither of us know anything, nor ever shall know anything. Is that other any the greater that his sharpness has been proved superior to mine? Is such a thing really worthy of our having sacrificed to it our rest at nights?'

"By main force I tore from my body the girdle of iron that encircled it, and resolved on the spot to renounce the worldly doings of this ascetic life, that I might seek peace in some quiet hut and in the pursuit of some useful occupation. And so I became a schoolmaster in a neighbouring village, and lived there quietly for several years that brought me neither joys nor sorrows.

"One day I had to make a journey to a distant village. When I arrived there in the evening, I saw a girl with a pitcher on her head, at sight of whom it seemed as if I wholly and completely burst into flames like the camphor that is burnt before the shrine of Siva.* After I had made the customary inquiries, I sued for this maiden's hand in marriage. I was rejected on the ground that I was too poor. Gone was the peace of my hut. I again took up business and worked as diligently as an ant. As soon as I had saved up something, I bought a golden bracelet and sent it to my adored one as a bridal present. She accepted it kindly, for she also loved me.

"Now it happened about this time that we had great floods, by reason of which the Ganges overflowed its banks to an extent never before known in the memory of man. The place, however, where I lived lay upon a hill.

"At night I went along the stream in order to see the rising of the waters. Then I saw lying on the bank a human form that had been floated down by the flood. It lay on its face and moaned. Full of sympathy, I sprang to its help, for the lower part of the body still lay in the water. As I bent over it, I saw that the hands were tightly clasped

* The third deity in the Hindu triad.

about a little case. At that moment greed came over me, sudden as a lightning flash. I thought, 'Here is thy marriage settlement.' And without once thinking of straightening myself up and reflecting (even as I half stooped I was transformed from a compassionate saver of human life to a murderous shore robber) I wrenched the case out of the hands that held it and rolled the body quickly back again into the water. As it rolled, the hair which had hitherto enveloped the entire head like a hood parted a little. Just then the moon emerged from behind a cloud, and I beheld the face of my beloved sweetheart.

"With a mighty effort I plucked the fainting form back out of the flood and threw myself down on the earth near her. Here I must have lain for quite a long time, like one bereft of his senses. Then the thought drove me to my feet, 'She will die here if you do not get help.' I took the heavy body in my arms and, by a superhuman effort, dragged myself to the nearest hut. Through the efforts of the good people there, who were more skilful than I, she came back to life. Meanwhile I slipped away to my lodging, for it would have been impossible for me to look her in the face.

"That night it was as if a storm-wind raged within me, tossing my heart ceaselessly to and fro. I did not know what to do; whether to fling myself into the flood where I would have cast her, or to throw myself at her feet, confess everything, and implore her pardon. Any third course did not seem to me to be possible. Ever tenser stretched the strings in this inward stress and struggle. One view seemed just to hold the balance with the other, until at last my brain, in this condition of forced equipoise, fell into a sort of stupor resembling sleep.

"I awoke with the thought, 'What, after all, is this love through attachment to which thou hast been willing to become a murderer, nay, hast become a murderer?' And in the light of this doubt I began to look sharply into this love, and suddenly I perceived its uncertainty and its misery. But I could now see clearly, because all the love in me had been burnt up in this one night, as a mighty conflagration in one night may burn up a whole forest. All others, however, when they think upon love, peer through the smoke and mist of the love that is present in them.

"Then there came over me, as it were, indignation, and I resolved to cast from me for ever this love to which I had hitherto clung so closely.

"On the morrow the entire village resounded with my fame, because, at the danger of my own life, I had saved my betrothed from death. I had become a hero, and the father of the girl came to me and said, 'Because you have saved my daughter's life, I give her to thee, and with her the due dowry. For she loves thee, and when the flood came, she took nothing but thy letter and thy bracelet and put them in that little case.'

"I could not answer a word, but turned away in silence; and because I saw some people just leaving the village, I hastily donned this red robe, took staff and calabash, and went with them.

"My thoughts were turned towards nothing but death. It was to me as if only through longing for death could I at all endure life. I clung to that longing. So soon, however, as I remarked that, I started, for I knew that all clinging brings suffering. I thought, 'What boots it that I have vanquished the lust of gold and the lust of fame and the love of woman, if now I cling to this thing death? How can I live serenely so long as there is aught to which I cling?'

"So I resolved to vanquish death also, even as I had vanquished these three. Therefore I ask once more, 'Does the venerable one know how one may vanquish death?'"

The old man smiled. "Remain here; sweep my hut; bring me fresh water; beg alms for me and speak no word. Do this for three years, and after that ask your question again!"

Gautama replied, "Venerable one, what good will that do me? How can I wait for three years? May not death come to-morrow, nay, to-day? I would vanquish him at once that I may at last have peace."

Then the old man smiled again and said, "Then go to the old man of the mountain!"

"Of what mountain?"

"Of Mount Meru!"

"How can I get there?"

"Only keep going along the banks of this sacred Ganges, until you come to where it springs out of a blue-gleaming cleft in a glacier. There you will see Mount Meru."

"But how shall I recognise it?"

"When you see it, it will see you."

"And how shall I recognise the old man of the mountain?"

"When he sees you, you will see him."

Gautama arose in silence, that he might, on the instant, enter upon his pilgrimage. The old man called after him—

"Only give heed to this, my son! When you have left behind you the haunts of men, you will come to wide wastes of sand and endless fields of snow. There you may wear your robe of red no more, nor speak aloud, nor take with you your calabash, else raging storms will fall upon your head. For, this you must know, 'Whoso turns against the realm of nature, against him also nature turns. But the wise man subdues her by his wisdom.' You may keep your staff, however."

Gautama promised to lay all this to heart.

Thereupon the old man again began, "One thing more, my son: When you have found Mount Meru, you can only reach it by going towards it with closed eyes. As often as you open your eyes, it will recede again to the horizon."

After Gautama had thus been informed of everything, he went forth boldly on his way.

When now he had been travelling many days, he came to the sacred city of Mathura. There stood the great image of Mahakala, which is otherwise known as Vishnu.* Sky-blue in colour, with four arms, it stood there four and twenty feet high, with naked paunch and teeth protruding like monstrous fangs. In its ears it wore snakes in place of rings, and two enormous snakes encircled its body. On its head it bore a crown of human skulls; around its throat a necklace of

* The second deity in the Hindu triad.

human skulls. From the elephant's hide, however, with which its back was covered, there fell drops of blood.

Now, when Gautama saw all the faithful who lay there rubbing their foreheads on the ground, he asked—

"Who is that?"

The people answered, "Do you not know Mahakala, the Mighty Lord of Time, the All-destroyer?"

"Is Mahakala death?"

"We do not know."

"Is Mahakala life?"

"We do not know."

"Why then do you pray to Mahakala?"

"We do not know. Our fathers prayed to him, and their fathers before them."

Then Gautama thought, "These are infatuated fools. I like not fools," and passed on his way.

When, again, he had been travelling many days, he came to Hastinapura, the elephant town. There, a powerful king reigned who had twenty thousand war elephants and a hundred thousand warriors. And the inhabitants of his city dwelt under his protection in plenty and in safety.

Now when Gautama entered the city and saw the garlanded houses, and on all hands heard the sounds of games and dance and song, he inquired what festival they were celebrating that day. The man whom he asked, however, answered—

"Stranger, our festivals are every day."

Meanwhile, a company of gaily-adorned young men and women came along the street. When they saw Gautama they said—

"Come with us, O stranger, to yonder shady wood."

But Gautama answered, "I cannot go to the shady wood while my task remains undone."

Thereupon they all laughed, and asked, "What sort of task have you got, you poor man?"

Then Gautama replied, "I want to go to Mount Meru, there to vanquish death."

They were filled with astonishment when they heard him say this, and each said to the other—

"He wants to go to Mount Meru, there to vanquish death!"

"Why do you bother yourself about death? Why do you wish to vanquish him?"

"Because I have desire for him, because I cling to him—therefore do I wish to overcome him."

When now Gautama saw how astounded they were, he asked—

"Will you also go with me to overcome death?"

"Stranger," they replied, "we have no time."

"What, then, have you got to do now?"

"We must dance the processional dance in the shady wood."

"And then?"

"Then we must bathe and anoint ourselves before the sun goes down."

"And then?"

"Then we must eat and drink."

"And then?"

"Then comes the night and its shining pleasures."

"And then?"

"Then we must bathe again and anoint ourselves and eat and make sport with our friends, and rest upon soft cushions in the breath of the breeze."

"And then?"

"Then we must again dance the processional dance even as now."

Then Gautama thought: "These are wise fools. I like not fools," and passed on his way.

When, again, he had been travelling for many days, he came to Indraprastha, the great ascetic grove. There he found a thousand holy men, who by powerful penances would fain have fought their way to the highest knowledge, for that is the ancient wisdom: "Knowing Brahman, he himself becomes Brahman."

One of them ate only stone-apples and the young shoots of trees. Another ate only one grain of rice a day, for, a fixed diet purifies. Another stood up to his hips in water day and night, and continually poured water over himself, for, water purifies. Another stood there motionless and stared into the sun's face with eyelids torn off, for, sunlight purifies. Another stood naked in the sun with four fires built up round him, for, fire purifies. Others again did other things. And thus in this grove such a mass of merit was heaped up by the pious penitents, that all the world wondered how the four quarters of the earth could continue to support the weight of this merit.

As Gautama approached this sacred assembly, the pious penitents asked him—

"Wilt thou also become one of us and practise the great penance?"

But Gautama answered—

"I have no time to tarry with you and to practise the great penance; I wish to go to Mount Meru, there to vanquish death."

"Venerable one," those penitents then replied, "indeed we also wish to vanquish death."

"How, then, would you vanquish death?"

"Even by becoming one with highest Brahman, for, 'Whoso himself is Brahman—him death no more compels.'"

"But how would you become one with that highest Brahman?"

"By the highest knowledge, for, 'Whoso knows Brahman, he is Brahman.' That is the ancient wisdom."

"But how would you attain to this highest knowledge?"

"By penitential practices and by reflection."

"Where, then, dwells that highest Brahman?"

"It dwells in us, venerable one; yea, in us. Even because of that is it said: 'Knowing Brahman, he becomes Brahman.'"

"Can you, then, see this highest Brahman in you with your eyes?"

"Nay, venerable one! How could the eye see Him through Whom it itself is the eye?"

"Then you are well able to perceive it with the understanding?"

"Nay, venerable one! How could the understanding perceive Him through Whom it itself is the understanding?"

"Then you are well able to feel it with the heart?"

"Nay, venerable one! How could the heart feel Him through Whom it itself is the heart?"

"But how now, O venerable ones? You see not this great Brahman with the eye, you perceive it not with the understanding, you feel it not with the heart. Whence, then, have you the knowledge that this great Brahman really is?"

"The rishis teach it."

"Then the rishis have perceived it and know that it is?"

"We believe so."

"And so you have desire for that highest Brahman?"

"How should we not? We long for Him as the wanderer for his home, as the weary eagle for its nest."

Then Gautama thought, "These pious men cling to that highest Brahman. Verily these pious men know not that all clinging brings pain. But must it not bring double pain when one clings to that of which he does not know whether it is or not? These holy men do not wish to overcome death, but only to escape him by hiding themselves in their own sophisms. They are foolish sages. I like not the foolish."

Thereupon he took his departure from thence.

After he had again been wandering many days, he came to those endless wastes of sand and those fields of snow of which the old man had told him, and he put away from him his red robe and his calabash. "How should I let forth spoken words from me here?" he thought, "since there is no one here with whom to hold speech?" He kept his staff however.

So he wandered on until he came to the place where the sacred Ganges breaks forth from a blue-gleaming cleft in a glacier.

And here he looked around for Mount Meru. He examined one after the other the mountain peaks that towered around him; each resembled every other in all particulars. Then one of the mountains, as his eye fell upon it, began to grow ever higher and higher, so that at last Gautama was obliged to throw his head far back in order to be able to look up to its summit, notwithstanding that the mountain lay far away on the horizon. Then Gautama knew that this was Mount Meru, and with long strides made towards it. But, no matter how fast he walked, he never came any nearer to the mountain.

Exhausted, he stopped to draw breath. Only then did the words of the old man occur to him—

"You can only reach it by going towards it with closed eyes."

But now the way led over boulders and past precipices. "How can I go on such a road with closed eyes?" thought Gautama. "I shall tumble into a ravine and be dashed to pieces."

He closed his eyes by way of trial, and carefully and anxiously groped his way forward. After a while he thought, "I will just take a little careful wink to see if I am any nearer yet to this mountain." But the mountain still stood there far away on the utmost horizon, and its summit towered so high that Gautama was obliged to bend his head far back in order to be able to see to the top. The mountain was tremendous to look at in its mantle of ice and snow that gleamed purple. But the clefts shone green like emeralds.

Again and again in like manner Gautama tried to advance towards it, but every peep he took revealed the mountain as far away as ever. At last desponding he sat down on the ground. "The old man has hoaxed me," was his thought. "For, even if I went on for seven whole days with my eyes shut, at the very moment when I opened my eyes the mountain would recede again to the horizon. On the other hand, if I keep my eyes closed, how shall I ever know whether I have reached it?"

Anger at the old man wholly mastered him. "Rascal!" he shouted, and shook his clenched fist.

And then the storm was upon him. From the mountain afar it came raging on, but to our Gautama it was as though it were roaring in his ears. He jumped up in terror. Not a single place anywhere around wherein to hide himself! And now the snow began to fall like the blossoms of the champak tree, and hailstones came down as big as mangoes.

Gautama turned around and threw himself flat on the ground. "Now," he thought, "it will blow me over into the abyss like a tuft of cotton from the bush. Very good! So be it!" And then suddenly all was deathly still. He got up. Mount Meru stood before him, notwithstanding that it ought now to have been behind him. "How wonderful!" thought Gautama. "I will follow the old man's counsel." And without once looking behind him to see if there might not be another Mount Meru still towering aloft in the old place, he closed his eyes and strode straight forward in the direction of the mountain, giving no thought to boulders or abysses, and immediately his mind within him became so strange, so still. Wholly at peace he walked on, and the road seemed suddenly to become as smooth as the path before his hut and as the sandy seashore at the ebb of the tide.

Then thought Gautama, "How splendid,

after all, are closed eyes! How wonderful that I never yet tried to go with closed eyes at home!" So he kept on walking quietly along, and never thought of the old man of the mountain nor yet of death, enjoying only his felicity.

At last he became weary and fell asleep as he walked, but only for as long as is needed to pass from the right foot to the left, or from the left foot to the right. But when he opened his eyes, it was to him as if he had slept through the whole night, and just in front of him there sat a little old man mending his clothes. Of the mountain, however, nothing more was to be seen.

Gautama thought, "I will ask him there whether he cannot show me the old man of the mountain."

Then the little man lifted his eyes and looked at him, whereupon Gautama saw that it was the old man of the mountain himself.

Meanwhile the man opened his mouth and said—

"Art thou there, Gautama?"

"Dost thou know me then?" asked Gautama.

The old man smiled. "I have known thee for countless thousands of years, but only by name. Wherefore dost thou come to me?"

"I would ask thee how one may vanquish death?"

The old man smiled again. "Hast thou yet vanquished the lust of gold?" he asked.

"Yes," replied Gautama.

"Hast thou yet vanquished the lust of fame?"

"Yes."

"Hast thou yet vanquished the love of woman?"

"Yes."

"Through what hast thou vanquished the lust of gold?"

"Through doubt."

"And through what hast thou vanquished the lust of fame?"

"Through doubt."

"And through what hast thou vanquished the love of woman?"

"Through doubt."

"Tell me."

Then Gautama began and again told his story.

When he had ended the old man nodded his head and said—

"Good, good, my son! Thou hast vanquished the lust of gold, thou hast vanquished the lust of fame, thou hast vanquished the love of woman. But hast thou yet vanquished life also? For else thou canst not vanquish death."

"I know not," answered Gautama. "What is life, my father? Show it to me. I would fain overcome it also."

"Thou art life."

"And what am I, my father?"

"Thou art the love of thyself. It thou must overcome before thou canst vanquish death."

Then Gautama stretched forth his arms so that the muscles stood out upon them and he said—

"Very good, my father, teach me. I am ready."

The old man still smiled. "Son," he said,

"thou hast done many deeds, but know that the highest lies not in doing, but in ceasing from doing."

"Have I not ceased from all, my father?"

"Thy ceasing is naught but a doing!"

"Then teach me, my father."

The old man gave him three doves which were black as night, with not a single white feather upon them.

"Come again to-morrow and tell me what thou hast seen on these."

Then Gautama took the three doves and departed thence. But his thought was:

"What have I to do with these three birds? They are black as night, and there is not a single white feather on them."

When he came to the old man next morning the latter said to him—

"Hast thou seen anything, my son?"

Then Gautama answered—

"Each of the three has got a white feather."

"Sadhu, my son! Have courage! Thou shalt yet vanquish death. This is the token thereof. Every day they will each get a fresh white feather, so wait in patience until the last black feather has gone. Then thou must eat all three birds. As soon as thou hast done that, come again to me. Then I shall be able to tell thee how thou mayst vanquish death."

This seemed to our Gautama a very easy task, and, light of heart, he departed thence.

So he waited day after day, and month after month, and year after year, and counted each fresh white feather. And, because he saw progress every day, he remained at peace and lived content and free from desires. At first, indeed, he thought: "Ah, if only the last black feather were gone!" But, when he had waited and watched and counted for three long years, this thought no longer came to him, and that was why he lived free from desires.

When now six years were come and gone and he was entering upon the seventh, almost all the black feathers were gone. And the three doves from day to day became ever more beautiful to look upon in their gleaming white feathers. Also they sat amicably all together and cooed to each other, whereas in the beginning they had often pecked at each other. Also they now began to sing, so wonderful to hear, whereas in the beginning they had only croaked hoarsely. And all day long Gautama stood and watched and peeped at them.

When now the day came upon which the last black feather had appeared, Gautama thought: "To be sure I came hither that I might vanquish death. But what boots it to rob these creatures of their lives? Were it not better that I contained myself in equanimity? Were it not better that I hold death even as life, and life even as death? Why should I strive? I am aweary of willing."

So he went over and opened the cage. The three doves fluttered out, encircled him three times, and thereupon soared straight aloft until they appeared only as tiny gleaming points, and then still higher soared until they quite disappeared in the blue ether.

Then Gautama thought, "I will go to

the old man of the mountain and tell him."

But when he came to the place, behold there was no old man of the mountain there; there was, however, a still lake which lay before his eyes like a mirror of crystal, and out in the middle there swam a crane. It sat motionless, and had its head hidden under its wings.

Gautama slipped down quietly to the water's edge, and looked out at the crane, and looked down to the very bottom of the lake, where the many-coloured pebbles lay and the white sand-grains with the nimble fish darting to and fro. And he felt so wonderfully at peace, so full of delight in his mind, that he thought within himself: "When was I ever so wonderfully at peace, so full of delight in my mind, as now when I sit by this clear lake, and see the sleeping crane and the many-coloured pebbles and the little fish down below. How sweet is peace!"

Thus he sat till the sun disappeared behind the mountains. Then he got up and went homewards, and although there was neither sun nor moon, yet he saw his way before him as if it had been day.

And next morning he stood before that old man in the hut. The old man smiled and said :

"Art thou there, Gautama? Hast thou vanquished death?"

"Venerable one," replied Gautama, "I have not vanquished him, because I could not eat those three doves. But what do I care about death? Death is to me even as life, and life is to me even as death. Venerable one, I live in peace, without discord."

"Tell me," said the old man. Then that Gautama began to tell what had happed to him upon his wanderings and when he was with the old man of the mountain. And when he had ended, the other said :

"Sadhu, my son! Thou hast vanquished death!"

Now when this Gautama came again to the cross-road and turned to the right into the high-road, there came from the other direction those others together with whom he had once left the village, and at this very same time they turned to the left into the high-road. And as they drew near to each other, those others greeted Gautama with much respect for they did not recognise him. All about them they carried sacks beneath the weight of which they groaned and sweated. But Gautama carried nothing but his stick in his right hand, and went along quietly and in comfort.

Whoso reads this story, let him know that that turning to the left when the others turned to the right signifies the love of solitude, and is the beginning of all that is good. For, as everything of the fruit nature requires warmth for its proper development, so everything in man that is good requires solitude that it may come to ripeness. The boundless plain around that stretched out like a smooth cloth—that is freedom from worldly thoughts; and the shadow is conscience. For, as it is only in the open plain that we can see the full measure of our shadow, no matter in what position the sun may be, so it is only in freedom from worldly thoughts that we experience the full power of conscience. And as at times our shadow lies behind us and at times runs before us, so conscience runs back and forth between the events of the past and the projects of the future.

The old man before the hut, whom Gautama saw when he lifted his eyes, is the voice of reason which always speaks so soon as the confusion and foolishness of what is worldly is stilled. The Ganges is the stream of human sufferings, up which he must go who strives for the highest, until he comes to the source, that is, to the origin of all sufferings. The red robe is the token of lust and sensuality, the calabash the sign of self-conceit and arrogance, and loud speech the sign of anger and hatred. All three must be laid aside by whoso passes beyond the haunts of men, that is, by him who would flee from the tumult and turmoil of the world out into the loneliness of the *I*. The staff is right thought. The storms and snowy weather are the voices of conscience, which here in these solitudes speak in tones of thunder what they only whisper among the abodes of men. As one who stops his ear with his finger hears the sounds in his body like a deafening uproar, so one who has closed his ears against the tumult of the world hears the voice of conscience resound within himself like thunder.

Mount Meru, however, is that holiest in us which is capable of raising us above ourselves. Gautama saw Mount Meru so soon as it saw him, and it grew before his eyes till it reached the zenith, and lay behind him as it also lay before him, all which means: This all-holy, so soon as we get sight of it, is known by us as verily the all-holy, and we see nothing else beside it. It fills up the entire field of our spiritual vision. Wheresoever we turn our gaze, there it is: there is nothing else beside it. And as Gautama could only reach Mount Meru with eyes closed—in sleep, so to speak—so we can attain this holiest in us, not by action and strain, but by letting go.

The old man of the mountain is the voice of this holiest within us, and as Gautama, when the old man saw him, saw also the old man and knew that it was the old man, so is it with the voice of this holiest within us. Its speech is truth, and at the same time the evidence of the truth of that which is spoken.

Word is here no longer mere formula or sign, but *being* itself.

The three black doves are self-ness in its threefold fundamental form of love for one's own *I*, ill-will against any other external *I*, and the delusion which represents these two as natural and justifiable. The gradual transition from black to white is the gradual dying out of this three-headed self-ness through a life of attentiveness and reflectiveness. In whomsoever this three-headed self-ness has died out—for him there is no longer any death. For as night is only present where day is present, and only so long as there is day, so is death only present where there is life, and only so long as there is life; but life is self-ness.

That crystal-clear mountain lake is the fruit and reward of that renunciation, of that letting go. As, however, that crane hid his head in his own feathers, so this letting go hides its reward in itself, is deed and the reward of deed in one, because it is the state of letting go.

He in whom the holiest is awake—he is inward light, hence he needs no outward light. Going homeward is this: As a man who has raised himself by a mighty upward leap must yet come back to earth again, so one who has raised himself above his own *I* must yet come back again to this *I*. But he brings somewhat with him of that from which he returns. And this is just the reason that he is greeted with respect, and that the others do not know him. That in going forth he turns to the left off the high-road, and in returning turns once more to the right into the high-road—this means that in the beginning he is as a fool in the eyes of men, but in the end, a sage and a saint.

ARCHITECT OF HIS FATE

IN Colombo, in the suburb of Kolupitiya, there lived a man named Nanda, who had neither parents nor brothers nor sisters, but who possessed something better than these, namely, the gracious memory of their love and of their virtues. Besides these, however, he had a friend and a sweetheart. His friend's name was Kosiya and his sweetheart's, Punna. The latter was observing a year of mourning for the death of her father, so that they had still some ten months to wait for their wedding.

One day, Nanda went alone to take a walk in the wood of coco-palms that lay along the shore. Cool and strong blew the ocean wind; low bowed the tops of the palm trees; in thunder broke the white-rimmed sea.

Our Nanda was in an extremely happy

frame of mind. As he walked quietly along he thought within himself, "Am not I the luckiest man in the world? Who else has such a friend, such a bride to be, so beautiful, so sensible, so pious, and both of them so true?"

Meanwhile he came to a clearing through which the wind blew gustily. And since here, almost the whole year round, the wind blew from the sea, the vegetation had assumed an extraordinary shape. It had only grown upon the side turned away from the wind.

Now our Nanda was in that state of inward equipoise, in which the merest trifle produces a profound effect upon us; he was in that condition in which a dog, sleeping in the sun, or a pair of kittens at play, may become objects of the greatest interest, and give rise to the deepest reflections, and so he came to a halt, pondering, before these strange-looking bushes.

"How truly great is the might of perseverance!" he thought. "Real strength lies in persistent endurance. Will my

Kosiya in friendship and my Punna in love thus persistently endure?"

All at once it seemed to him that he as good as knew nothing if he did not know this. In that moment he fell into man's great vice—the vice of sacrificing the flowing cup of the present and the treasure-house of the past, in order to filch a tiny crumb from the future; no, not to filch any such crumb, for the future will elude no man and no man will elude the future. Yet, just to get this tiny crumb a little bit earlier, they give up their all. The whole of philosophy, which teaches man to stand still under the hammer of necessity, they surrender for the petty arts of the soothsayer and the fortune-teller.

He began to brood. "Certainly," ran his thought, "my good fortune is great, but it would be still greater good fortune if only I knew that it was going to last. I must devise some test for this."

So he thought and thought, until the setting sun warned him that it was time to turn homewards.

The whole night through he was kept from sleeping by this one thought. At long last, with the morning light his plan took shape. At one stroke he would put to the test the faithfulness both of betrothed and of friend. He would go a long journey as if upon urgent business, and during his absence would entrust his bride to the care of his friend. Neither of them as yet had seen the other, for his friend led a life of solitude. More and more absorbed did he become in his plan. It was now no longer a question of, *Would he or not?* it was only a question of *How?* A voice within him spoke in warning, "Why stake all your happiness upon a single card?" But already the madness was too strong upon him. Even the prospect of a lengthy separation from his beloved no longer had power to dismay him.

When he thought his plan sufficiently worked out in all its details, he betook himself to his friend Kosiya at Bambalupitiya.

The latter lived in a little house flanked by a couple of banana trees, and led up to by two wooden steps. Kosiya fared rather scantily. In the morning he ate a cake of rice which he bought at the baker's for a halfpenny. At noon he ate a dish of rice and a little vegetable curry, and in the evening, he took what was left over, along with a couple of bananas. At all meals his only drink was pure spring water.

Thus he lived, a diligent reader of the Suttas,* and fully occupied with the work of reflecting upon himself. For he had seen and understood that all good here below is comprehended in the avoiding of evil, and that evil is only overthrown by reflection, is consumed in it as camphor in fire, naught remaining, not even ashes.

"My work," he would say, "does not lie in doing, but in refraining from doing."

One day Nanda said to him, "You live like a monk. Why do you not enter the Order of the Exalted One? You would live more comfortably."

With a smile, Kosiya replied: "Because I am a glutton; that is why I do not enter

* The Discourses of the Buddha.

the Order of the Exalted One. My stomach demands an evening meal."

The brothers of the Order of the Buddha may not partake of food after noon.

"Moreover," Kosiya continued, "I am vain. I could not endure to go about with shaven head." And, indeed, he had a head of hair so full and long, and withal so fine and glossy, as was possessed by scarcely another in Colombo, and he wore it after the old fashion, coiled up high, with a comb of tortoise-shell stuck in it. "For," he would say, "that was the way of our fathers, and ought not to be laid aside except under necessity." For the rest, he was strong and tall of stature, with serious, regular features, and at this time might have been somewhere about the beginning of the thirties in age.

Moreover, he had not always lived as a recluse, but had passed his earlier years like other young fellows, and had been through more than a few love adventures. All at once, after a certain night of revelling, he had become this present Kosiya.

Nanda once was sitting in the shade, reading an English book.

"What sort of book is that you are reading?" Kosiya asked.

"What sort of book should it be?" answered Nanda. "Love! love! As always, nothing but love! Just as you came, they were kissing and fondling one another and enjoying the keenest delight; but I'll wager you, on the very next page they will both be lamenting in the deepest despair. What a madness is this, which impels us again and again to inflame our fancy with these imaginings! It sometimes seems to me as if we played with these love-images over and over again, only in order that we may not perceive the reality—I mean, death. For, confess it yourself, what hinders us from clear thinking more than love?"

"Nanda," said the other, "what a way to talk! I see you, I hear your voice, and yet it is as if it were some one else speaking! Truly it is a frenzy, an intoxication that has taken possession of us all. Is not intoxication intoxication? Is not one kind of intoxication equally as disgraceful as any other? We deride and despise a person who has become a child through the inebriation that comes of indulgence in wine, but we ourselves every day become childish again through the inebriation of love! Nanda, ought we not to try to become sober? Ought not the pleasures of sobriety to have as great charms for us as the pleasures of drunkenness? And can I not better enjoy every pleasure when my understanding is clear and my brain vigilant? Simply out of desire for increased enjoyment, ought we not to become sober and shun drunkenness? Ought we not to train ourselves in sober thinking, as the athlete trains the muscles of his arms and legs? Nay, ought we not to be much more ardent than he, since our goal is so much the more important? Nanda, your words have brought light to me! This very day I make a beginning!"

"Dear Kosiya," began Nanda, "for me, I much fear me, it is all too late to begin the career of an athlete in sobriety. You must know, my friend, since yesterday I have fallen in love past all redemption. From that circumstance alone springs my present disgust at this love story. I cannot see her again until to-morrow. How shall I pass the time till then? I would almost have despaired, and actually thought of death. Finally, in my distress I seized this book, and then you came. Forgive me that I have unintentionally lured you along a false track."

"You call that a false track! Do you really think that, as a drunken man, you are capable of distinguishing what is true from what is false?"

"Oh, if you knew Punna! There is none like her in all the world. Follow my example, Kosiya!"

"What's the use of the whole world, of me included, falling in love, when you have already appropriated the best beforehand?"

"Don't mock! Follow my example, Kosiya! There is only one real happiness in the world. If only you knew what true love is! Ah, if I could only remain for ever in this delightful drunkenness!"

"Nanda, I now see with my own eyes how great is the danger. Hitherto I have known it only by hearsay. It is to me as if something were emitted from you like the breath from a drunken man. Since I am not yet inebriated like you, I will try first the worth of soberness, for I think it is easier to turn one's self from being a sober man to being a drunkard, than to turn from being a drunkard to being a sober man. Hence, if I don't find sobriety to my taste, drunkenness is still left to me!"

"But, dear Kosiya, can a sober man and a drunkard remain friends?"

"Our friendship, my Nanda, will become stronger than ever. For, the man who has become sober is more capable of true friendship than he was before, and the drunkard stands more than ever in need of him."

Thus did the two friends shake hands upon a bond of friendship for life, and thus from this hour onwards did Kosiya begin his life of sobriety. He had now lived it for more than three years, and when Nanda would jestingly ask him—

"Now, friend, is not sobriety a rather tasteless dish?" he would answer thoughtfully—

"It tastes pure. It is the only dish that tastes pure."

Nanda, on the other hand, in the winning of his Punna, had come through a year of torment and agitation, until finally a few months ago he had succeeded in securing her promise to be his bride. The death of her father postponed the date of their marriage, and Nanda was left with sufficient leisure in which to revel in dreams of future bliss. We have seen how he was minded to employ this leisure.

Entering Kosiya's house, he found him seated cross-legged on the floor of the back veranda, attired in an immaculate white jacket and loin-cloth. He was busily engaged studying a palm-leaf manuscript.

After due greetings, Nanda began—

"Would it not be better, friend, if you again began to mix a little among men?"

In some surprise Kosiya looked at him. Nanda went on—

"You will end by completely dying out in yourself." But then, "Oh dear!" he cried, "there, I've gone and put my foot in it! Your precise aim is to die out!"

"It is not dying out that is our goal," answered Kosiya, "but a life free from desire and craving. Cessation follows of itself, as darkness follows when the light burns itself out."

"Kosiya, I am not a clever talker. If I were to go on talking with a hidden object in view, I would be sure to make a bungle of it. So I will just say to you straight out; you must do me a favour."

"Most willingly, friend, if it is in my power."

"Oh, you won't be asked to give me money or put in a word for me anywhere. This is quite within your power and is quite simple. The thing is this. When I was walking yesterday on the shore and came to the clearing where the wind-twisted shrubbery grows, the thought came to me that real strength lies in constancy. Hence the strength of love also must rest in constancy. Hence, also, the greatest love must be that which is the most constant. I thought further, 'How can I make sure whether my Punna's love will prove constant or not?' And all at once it seemed to me that all the world was worth nothing to me if I could not discover this. So I resolved to put her to the test, and have pondered over it the whole night through, and finally came to the conclusion that this can only come about through you. For you are true, and will never do anything unworthy of our friendship. To be brief, I will go upon a lengthy journey, and in the mean time you shall pay court to her, and do everything seemly that a man may do to make a woman fall in love with him. If she stands this test, I will be completely satisfied, and henceforth believe that I enjoy the greatest happiness possible upon earth."

Kosiya was silent for a space; then he began—

"Friend Nanda, I am only some two

years older than you. I am not sure if it is exactly my place to tender you advice; all the same, I think you had better abandon your scheme."

"But why?" cried Nanda, warmly.

"Because it is not the straight way. Whoso puts crooked questions to Fate ought not to be surprised if he receives crooked answers."

"What do you mean by your *crooked* and *straight?* What else do I want to do, but assure myself of the faithfulness of my betrothed? This is the straight road to that end."

"All right! Let it be that it is the straight road, the question remains, 'Is it necessary that you should go this straight road?' It is not necessary that a road should be followed simply because it is a straight one."

"Kosiya, believe me, if ever I am to enjoy peace of mind in this life, I must make this test. Is it not a friend's duty to give peace of mind to his friend?"

"There we come to the other side of the

business. You say it is quite simple and is quite within my power. To be sure, you require from me neither money nor recommendations, but you ask for my own *I*. I am to give up my own peace, the care of my own *I*, in order to bring about your peace."

"Can you not sacrifice your peace for a paltry couple of weeks out of love for your friend?"

"Do you not know that the Exalted One teaches—

> 'Turn not aside from thine own goal
> For others, be they ne'er so great!'"

"Your speech is not particularly like a friend's. But do you seriously think that it will endanger your wellbeing, if you make believe to pay court to a woman for a few weeks?"

Thus he went on pleading and urging, with all the more vehemence the more the other resisted.

Then an idea occurred to Kosiya. He thought, "How can my friend's love be perfect, if even now he raises doubts as to the faithfulness of his betrothed? Will he ever be certain? Will he not continually torture himself? For there are some men to whom all those good things bring only torment, which to others are a source of joy. Would it not be right that I should make the attempt to bring him also that secure peace of mind, free from desiring, which I have myself enjoyed these last few years?"

In this guise did vanity insinuate itself into Kosiya's heart; thus did he forget his own weal that he might take upon himself the burden of his friend's wellbeing.

He began. "If you really insist upon it I will do as you wish. Only you must promise me that you will stay away for at least three months, and also, in case the results of the test do not correspond with your expectations, that you will try to keep calm and lend your ear to exhortation."

Filled with pleasure, Nanda fell on his neck.

"I promise everything. Only, during the three months that I am away, you must write to me often."

"Once a month is enough, my friend. You will hear from Punna much oftener than that."

"Good, good! My best of friends! This very day I will take you to her, and to-morrow I start off. It will be best that you come with me now."

Thus toils the fool at the overthrowing of his fortune, even more zealously than he had laboured at its up-building.

On their way to Punna Kosiya began again—

"I see three possibilities, Nanda. I might see four of them, if at the same time you would like to put your friend also to the test."

Nanda coloured up on the instant; but Kosiya did not notice, for he was looking straight ahead of him.

"Which three possibilities do you mean?"

"The first is, that her love remains true to you. In that case, all is well, at least for you. The second is, that she does not remain true. In this case all may be made well. The third is, that we may fall mutually in love with one another."

Our Nanda began to feel uncomfortable. "How you talk!" he said, "I feel quite sure of you."

"No man is sure but he who shuns temptation. What is to be done in the last eventuality? In that case she will belong to you by right, and to me by nature."

"Punna belongs to me, and to no one else."

Kosiya threw a side glance at him. They were now in front of the house.

"Nanda, friend," he again began, "would you not rather leave this business alone? Time will teach you more surely than any test, whether or no your dear one is true to you."

"Oho! Do you think I am afraid you will cut me out?" he laughed, at the same time knocking rather loudly at the door.

The Tamil servant opened it. They entered the reception room where they found present both mother and daughter. The mother, a venerable-looking matron, was a cripple, and remained seated in a big Indian basket-work chair.

Somewhat hurriedly, Nanda informed his betrothed that he must start next morning upon a long journey. Kosiya's presence seemed to be grateful to him, since it saved him from the first outbreak of surprise on his sweetheart's part. In accordance with the demands of etiquette, Punna listened in silence. Only a light "Oh!" came from her lips.

After a brief interval, Kosiya took his departure, so as not to intrude upon the scene of parting. But before he went, Nanda, with a certain impressiveness, made him pledge himself to visit Punna at quite frequent intervals. In parting, Nanda shook his hand with such force that it hurt.

I will not paint the parting scene between Nanda and Punna; so many writers, skilled in the picturing of emotions, have described the most touching farewell scenes, that the reader may just pick out himself what he thinks is the best of them, and insert it at this part of my narrative. For, if manners in the East and in the West differ somewhat from one another, yet lovers are alike all the world over.

So, next morning early, Nanda set off to Madras on the mainland. It happened to be exactly the first day of September.

I would have it understood, that the only letters which will be exhibited in full are those from Kosiya to Nanda; that those from Punna to Nanda will be given only in part, and those from Nanda to Punna not at all. For what publisher could undertake to publish all the scribblings of lovers?

Already, on the seventh of September, Kosiya received the following note:

"Madras, 4th September.

"DEAR KOSIYA,—

"I am eagerly awaiting a letter from you. What do you think of Punna?

"THY NANDA."

To this Kosiya replied as follows:

"Colombo, 8th September.

"DEAR NANDA,

"Please bear in mind that it is part of our agreement that I am to write to you only once a month. So, have patience! Besides, what can I write to you so soon already? I as yet know no more than my eyes, and the eyes of everybody else for that matter, must tell them, that your betrothed is perfectly beautiful—so perfectly beautiful that one can say nothing further than just, 'She is perfectly beautiful.' She possesses that peculiar type of beauty which is more frequently found amongst the Hindus than among the Sinhalese. However, you are perhaps still in a position to be able to call to mind from former times, that beauty is a property which your intended possesses in common with many another woman. Beauty alone, especially such perfect beauty, is, for a man of understanding and experience, no ground whatever for falling hopelessly in love. So I suppose that your adored one possesses certain specific excellences which for you make her unique, but which I in this short space of time have so far been unable to discover. So you must have patience until the end of the month, when my first letter is rightly due. This present epistle I shall be gracious enough not to include in the reckoning, since it really contains nothing that has to do with our agreement.

"So farewell! and bear in mind the promises you made me.

"THY KOSIYA."

Punna to Nanda.

"My best beloved Nanda,

"I am still as if stupefied. When I awoke this morning early, my pain was greatest. I woke up with a sorrowful sensation in my heart, but knew nothing of yesterday. Then, like a flash of lightning, memory returned, and I felt so lonely in my heart, so sick to death. I cannot describe it to you. It seemed to me as if everything in me was all burnt up and could never, never grow again. 'How shall I live through this day?' was my thought. But it now seems to me, that the best way to teach any one to endure is to lay upon them a still heavier burden. For, when evening came, and the time returned in which you have always been with me, then I wished that the morning were back again, which at least had the day behind it.

"It is now time to go to sleep, but I cannot. My relief must be this letter.

"Beloved, I cannot write any more. I have sat up long into the night. I feel as if all my senses were frozen. Nanda, I think that if you loved me as I love you, there would not be any business in the world of sufficient importance to tear you away from me for three months.

"Dearest, in spirit I now say good-night

to thee. I feel thy hand on mine. How gently you stroke it! Ah, how painful happiness can be!

"THY PUNNA."

"Colombo, 8th September.

"MY ONLY BELOVED NANDA,

"I have read both letters with the sweetest emotions. I carry them about with me and keep on reading them and reading them, although I knew them both by heart long ago. Beloved, how comes it that my greatest comfort is to know that you also suffer? What a peculiar thing is the torment of love!

"You ask me if I have wept. Alas, Beloved! I am such a foolish girl. I know well that weeping is useless. Our religion teaches it so often. But the comforts of religion at present appear to me so unsatisfying, so useless, as if not meant for us at all. You must not think, however, that I go about all the day with streaming eyes. I must let you know frankly that tears came to my eyes just twice, but then I thought of the promise that I gave you, and I crushed them down again.

"You ask if your friend has visited me often. He was here the day after your departure, before I had written the first letter. I quite forgot to tell you. Yesterday he was here again. Every time that my sorrow allows me the opportunity, I have wondered why you wish him to call so often. I have just a little suspicion that in him you have placed a spy upon me, but do not think, beloved, that I say that in earnest.

"I will privately confide to you that I hope for a letter from you to-morrow again. I cannot think of it without my heart leaping.

"THY FOOLISH PUNNA."

"Colombo, 26th September.

"MY ONLY DEAREST,

"You complain that, since your departure, I have only written four letters to you, and that I do not tell everything I do and suffer through the day with sufficient detail. Believe me, dearest, the whole day is spent in telling you what I do and suffer. I speak only to thee. To others I speak only as a puppet to puppets. But it is so difficult to write down what one feels. It is so cold looking, so lifeless. I am afraid my letters give you a very poor idea of my love for you.

"For your friend, who at first was an object of indifference to me, and then—forgive me—somewhat tiresome, I am beginning to feel thankful to you. He has been here several times; his latest visit was last night. We spoke continually of you. Last night we happened by chance to speak of the views of philosophers concerning love. He is going to tell me something about it out of a book next time he comes. He maintains that it is not good for people to continue in grief and sadness. He holds that it is not distraction but thinking about pain that is the best cure for pain. What an extraordinary idea! Altogether, he holds very peculiar views, but many a time I half think that he is right. For, when I am almost sick with longing, and I think strongly of the object of my longing—guess who that is—it seems to me as if I found relief. But I frankly believe that he meant it quite another way.

"Ah, my beloved, how I long for thee!

"THY PUNNA."

Kosiya to Nanda.

"Colombo, 30th September.

"MY DEAR NANDA,

"I imagine that you have been expecting a letter from me these last few days. But I will not tease you, I know that you have been counting the days.

"When I think that one-third of the testing time has passed, I must frankly admit that so far I have not done very much; indeed, up till now I have been unable to arrange any test. During the first few days, your intended was insensible in her grief to all external influences. At the very outset I had to find some means of calling her attention to my existence. This I succeeded in doing by speaking continually about you. In this way she grew accustomed to me, but it was a long time before the waves of the pain of parting had subsided. Only lately did I succeed in making a little progress, by passing from love as it reigned between a certain Nanda and a certain Punna, to love in general. From this position I think I shall be able to make a safe advance. I shall pose as a despiser of love and of its joys, and in this I shall be all the more successful, seeing that, as you know, I shall here be saying what I really feel. For my part, I frankly feel that, in this domain, it is out of place to amuse one's self and practise deception, and I also know that later on I shall receive my punishment for it, but I comfort myself with the thought that I am doing it all in the service of friendship.

"My plan is this. This contempt for love must call forth from her a rebuttal. She will begin to fight against me. But that is a sort of lover's sport. For, love also is nothing else but a fight, which is to be distinguished from other fighting only in this, that the pleasure derived from it is found, not so much in victory, as in the fight itself and in submission. Victory and defeat here signify much about the same thing and are both equally sweet. Hence, where two fight with one another, even to the point of mutual hatred, they only, as it were, prepare the soil of love. Indifference only is the death of love.

"I now expect, however, unless she is quite different from all other feminine creatures, that she will try to convert me, not only by words but also by deeds; in a word, my hope is, that in order to convince me of the falsity of my ideas, she will attempt to make me fall in love with her myself. Every girl, every woman thinks that she can venture on this in perfect safety, because she knows herself to be only jesting. But in love, jest only too often passes unnoticed into earnest; the deceiver becomes a deceived deceiver, and cannot find his way back again. I know that the truth of this law may be demonstrated, not only in women, but also in men; and amongst these latter in a certain one called Kosiya. But my safety lies precisely in this, that I *know* that this is the case.

"You see, my good Nanda, that I am zealous about the work. Perhaps you are wondering at my zeal. To-day I only want to let you know that I shall carry out my plan. Oh, I hope that everything will turn out all right for you, for me, and perhaps also for her. At all events, so much in her is steadfast, that this is the only art and fashion from which I promise myself any result. In case, however, you think that a test of this kind is against our agreement, just let me know, and we will give up the whole affair. For I can inform you that nothing is to be done with your betrothed by the usual methods, by flattery and lover-like languishings. She would only laugh at such things, for she is sensible to a high degree and has a rare turn for logical thought. In one word, she is sound through and through and inaccessible to any sickly sentiment. The only point where she is vulnerable is, as said, in that love of battle which every healthy person possesses, so long as he has not had it dried up within him through reflection.

"In order to complete the picture of your beloved, I must add that she is discreet, and does not appear to be conscious either of her beauty or of her rare virtues. The crown of all, however, I consider to be her good-natured inoffensiveness, which is always inclined to see and to think the best of everybody—a quality exceptionally rare among clever women, the which, however, I feel disposed to prize more highly than all other excellences taken together.

"So much for one day.

"Best wishes and greetings,

"FROM THY KOSIYA."

"Punna to Nanda.

"Colombo, 9th October.

"MY BELOVED NANDA,

"I really do not know how to write letters properly, but I know very well how to read them—that is, your letters; of others I know nothing. What was troubling your mind when you wrote your last letter? Have you met with some annoyances in the affairs that have called you away to Madras, or have I unwittingly said something to cross you? Dearest, do tell me what it is! I am so disquieted. Ah, if only your business were all finished and I only had you back with me again! Do you still remember that evening when we sat together, a short time before your departure, and a big fire-fly alighted on my shoulder, so that suddenly in the darkness we could see one another's faces? Do you still remember how at that moment we smiled to each other? Ah, dearest, best beloved, how could I ever possibly live without you? Only come soon, come soon! Oh, I can still remember a whole host of such glances, and I would not exchange one of them for a kingdom! I am looking for you every day, every day.

"Alas, beloved! What a terrible thing is parting to lovers! But ought we then to misunderstand one another? Wert thou here, one glance would make everything right. You reproach me that at the beginning of my letter I say—'I speak only like a puppet to puppets,' and then at the end—'I had an animated conversation with your friend Kosiya.' Dearest Nanda, we have always spoken of nothing but of thee. He told me so many beautiful things about you. I was so grateful and loved you so much. Only once did we wander from you, to speak of the views of the philosophers about love. It came in quite appropriately. Indeed, I think it was myself that turned the conversation in that direction, and your friend then began to unfold his own views on the subject. Only think, dearest! He holds love in contempt. He seeks some standpoint superior to love. I only laughed. As if there were any standpoint higher than love! What do you think, Nanda? Is not that the highest standpoint which yields the highest happiness? And is not love the highest happiness? Would it not be a triumph for our love to lead this unbeliever back to love? For, I refuse to believe that any one can be by nature a foe to love. Certainly he also formerly thought otherwise. But, dearest, if you think that I should not engage any more in such conversations, just write to me so at once. I will stop it at once and tell him—'Nanda does not like it.'

"With longing I await a letter from thee.

"THINE EVER FAITHFUL PUNNA."

"Colombo, 18th October.

"Dearest, how long you have kept me waiting and then what a cruel letter! Ah, have pity! You say that the disquietude which I feel is not the result of your letter, for your letter was written with feelings entirely unchanged. How cold! But the disquietude lay in myself. Ah, perhaps you are quite right, my Nanda. Truly I am tormented with disquietude day and night by reason of your absence. It seems to me as if I have been more quiet before than I am now. I am so sad and miserable all the day. Yesterday evening your friend was here. He comes mostly in the evenings. He has such a peculiar way of rousing me and provoking me to contradict him. He speaks of love, hope and happiness as coldly as if he were teaching mathematics. He is a remarkable man. I believe I have already convinced him on several points, but I am not yet quite sure. This I think I ought to tell you. At first, however, I did not want to, but because you want to hear everything I tell it also to you. Your friend has just read me bits out of the Suttas * about love. He clearly proved to me that, wherever life is recognised to be suffering, love is the worst of all things, since it fetters us for ever to life and at the same time to suffering. At first I shrank a little. But then I thought, and told him, 'That all life is suffering I know quite well, just because all life is transitory. But that love is the best thing in the world—this I know just as surely. And the Exalted One himself cannot abate my belief.' Then he laughed, and said that I reasoned just the way all women reason. But what harm is there in that? My pride it is just that I am a woman. But then he began to paint the greatness of solitude and of the recluse. He called him the only freeman: all others were the slaves of love. He compared him with the sun, and made use of such words and images, that I could do nothing but sit and listen to him in admiration. But do not imagine that I allowed him to see anything of it. After all they are only ideals that he sets forth—ideals which neither your friend nor any one else in the world can ever realise. My

* Portions of the Pāli Buddhist Scriptures.

Nanda, have you ever reflected upon love from this point of view? But what a silly question to ask!

"How splendid is this night, so dark and so luminous! I am in such a mood of foreboding, like one who looks upon something vast! And is not this splendour something vast! Ah, if only you were sitting beside me! But I feel quite serene and happy, exactly as if you really were sitting beside me. It seems as if the night-wind gave me tidings of thee. Only come back soon, my Nanda, and stroke my hand again as you used to do.

"THY FAITHFUL PUNNA."

Kosiya to Nanda.

"Colombo, 31st October.

"DEAREST FRIEND,

"Everything has gone exactly as I had anticipated. She has taken up the challenge. She is trying to convert me. I would scarcely have known that she was a woman if this womanly trait had not at last come to light. How moving she is! Her coquetry is even more natural than the naturalness of coquettes. Nanda, if I carry this test through to a finish and in the process do not myself fall in love, I am a rascal. What torments me always is the doubt if I am doing right, but I will tell you later, dearest friend, what in reality drives me on. Oh, how splendidly everything may turn out.

"I have just been reading out to her some passages from the Suttas about love. I invited her to make the deductions that follow upon the law, 'All life is suffering,' as it affects love. I am aware that I was merciless, and showed no sympathy with her anguished fluttering. When she no longer knew what to do to save herself, she took a defiant leap over the boundaries of logic, away into that domain in which no rules any longer hold good. But when I then began to speak of the greatness of solitude, I saw clearly by her shining eyes how she felt and understood along with me. How I envy thee such a noble heart! Marriage is not for her. She is quite capable of comprehending the highest in the teaching of the Blessed One. When I promised you to put her to the test, I did so because I did not know her. Now I continue just because I do know her! Perhaps a double benefit will flow from my action. I speak in riddles; but only have patience, my best of friends!

"You naturally will know if there is actually anything happening. What shall I say? I only have certain impressions. The only thing that does not seem to be quite right is this—that she has denied herself to me for the last two or three days.

The servant said that she was ill, that she was in bed. But I heard in the next room the rustling of her robe. I cannot have been mistaken.

"That is about all that I have to tell you to-day. I have forgotten something. Her coquetry does not run in the direction of changes in her dress, flowers, perfumes, etc., as you may perhaps imagine. Oh no! Punna is far above such devices. It was only a coquetry of thought, a sort of dwelling upon points where one had expected more rapid progress. Somewhat as if a musician should coquet with his theme, and by some fresh transposition bring it once more in a fresh form to the astonished ear.

"But enough! If I go on chattering like this, you will have good right to say that I am already in love, and that thus the fourth of my possibilities has come to pass. But I place reliance in the fact that I see each step I take.

"Farewell, my only friend."

Punna to Nanda.

"Colombo, 2nd November.

"MY GOOD NANDA,

"You keep impressing on me again and again that I am to let you know every little thing that occurs every individual day. I am doing so faithfully. I cannot do more than I am already doing. You distress me with your insistence. If you only knew how scattered are my thoughts! How can I seize all of them? I am restless as I have never been before in all my life. You ask if, perhaps, my intercourse with your friend has not something to do with it. That means: You think it might perhaps be as well if I dismissed him. But why, my Nanda? I really do not know why. Let him keep on coming; it does not trouble me. I mean—do not take me up wrongly—he speaks of high things which must trouble every thinking being. I am really telling you everything. Last night I was not able to see him because I was ill; that is to say, not so ill that I had to lie down—you need not be anxious about me—but I only had an indisposition which will soon pass away. On the whole, if you should think anything—but what am I saying? My Nanda, and jealous? Dearest, I have trust only in thee. It seems to me as if I hated this Kosiya. I hate this cold calculator, this so—I do not know what to say, but you know him better than I do. But I speak so, just in case this may have something to do with my unrest. But really, what silly stuff I am writing!

"My Nanda, think, think always of me, as I shall make it my principal occupation to think of thee.

"THY FAITHFUL PUNNA."

"Colombo, 13th November.

"Dear heaven, Nanda, how shall I write to you if you take up my words that way? What is this that you have made out of my harmless expression, that thinking of thee is my principal occupation? For the expression is really harmless. Alas! Alas! and yet—O miserable me! But you dare not make out of it what you have made out of it. How can you know that it is now a toilsome occupation for me to think of you? But perhaps there was something in my letter that you have misread. It was written so badly. Alas, I really do not know! But surely, Nanda, that is not just. No! And I think that justice is the first thing I must require from my future husband. I do not think that I could love any one who is not just. Oh, what a mad woman I am! Forgive me, forgive me! I cannot write another word. As soon as I can I will write more. I think I must write you something. I must indeed.

"THY UNHAPPY PUNNA."

"Colombo, 22nd November.

"Alas, Nanda, your words are sharper than daggers in my heart. I convert anyone to the happiness of love? Unfortunate that I am! Who was it that taught me that love was the greatest happiness? It is the greatest torture! O Nanda, you know all.

But if you only knew how I suffer; how every night I sob and cry! Oh, I ought to have told you long ago. But what? What? Oh what is going to happen? Where shall I find comfort? In religion? How shall I look in religion for something which I can only find in myself? But if I had had religion in me I should never have come to this, for the Exalted One has shown us clearly what is to be avoided. I cry for comfort and find none. O Nanda, my dear beloved, my delight, my only happiness, where art thou? Only stay! Oh, I stretch out my arms to you. Come, I will fly to thy breast. Woe is me, I am raving! Oh how I hate dissimulation! More than poison, more than death! I might be at peace if only I knew that I was now at least speaking without dissimulation. Oh if only you had never gone away! Is that true? Oh, my brain is turned. I know nothing, only that I am the most unfortunate of women."

Kosiya to Nanda.

"Colombo, 24th November.

"My Nanda,

"Friend I may not any longer call you—my fate has overtaken me. I write this because my members do their service out of old use and habit, but inwardly I am as one mangled, crushed flat beneath the iron wheels of Fate. My foolishness and my presumption are to blame for everything.

"The third month is not yet completed but the game is over. It all happened this way. When day after day I could not get to see her, I became impatient. My fancy began to work. I thought that she withdrew herself from me because love was beginning to work. Presumptuous that I was! At last I began to watch the house. One day when I saw the servant go off to the bazaar I knocked at the door. She opened it herself. I knew well that she must open it herself. In that moment, as her glance met mine, I felt that my fate was sealed for ever. A peculiar gleam was in her eye, such as I had never seen there before. She seemed to me to be a little thinner. She must have suffered. I felt how my heart clave to her and I stood there like a culprit. Never in all my life have I felt at once so happy and so miserable. I talked a few stupid commonplaces for which I could have kicked myself. Certainly the loss of inward assurance is, for the man, a much more serious loss than for the woman, because, with the latter, helplessness may only give her a fresh charm; the man, however, it only makes laughable or contemptible.

"I begged her to let me call again. She

agreed with perfect simplicity. So I saw her again, saw her more often than ever. She remained perfectly calm and dignified. I, on the contrary, behaved like a boy, like a fool. I spoke at the wrong time, and was silent at the wrong time, and my speech, like my silence, said only one thing: 'I love thee!' Oh how ashamed I was of this shameless openness! But, what was worse, my former impudent assurance of her love for me, in the face of her present behaviour, became ever more and more turned into doubt. All my self-confidence was gone. Day after day I was mercilessly tossed hither and thither. I groaned at the caprices of women. To-day I know that it was not their caprices that tortured me but my own foolishness. I in fact saw everything only through the frenzy of my love.

"At last, yesterday, I could bear it no longer. So, in a sort of despair, I made my venture. I knew I was betraying my friend, ruining my own future in this and in the next life, and insulting perhaps the noblest woman that lives. But nothing mattered. That is precisely the madness of love. What I said or did I do not know, for I was out of my senses. But, Nanda, you ought to have seen the dignity and kindness with which she refused me. O Exalted One, what cloistered quiet is deep enough ever to lead me to forget that scene? She was as a goddess to me.

"The betrayed betrayer am I, Nanda. I am he who, from the safe shore of reflectiveness, ventured out upon the high seas of love, and there, seized by a whirlwind, was no longer able to make his way back again. Believe me, she herself did nothing but fight out the honourable contest into which she was lured by my cunning. On me lies all the blame.

"Nanda, I will confess everything to you. When you came into the quiet of my hut and pressed me to play a part towards your intended, it was my duty, the duty of the reflective man, to convince you by reasoning of the foolishness of your plan. But I allowed myself to be led away by presumption. I thought, 'If I cause the betrothed of this my only friend to be unfaithful to him, I shall be able to lead him also into this serene peace which I myself now so fully enjoy.' Fool that I was! I had nothing but a look, ever the same, in the mirror of my pride. It was thus that I departed from that first rule of prudence in all virtue—to shun temptation. Thus did I fling heedlessly away my own spiritual good, in order—perhaps!—to save thine. Once more, Fool that I was! How did I know what your good was, whether, indeed, it might not lie precisely in love? For, as through a gateway, through love also may well lie the road to Nibbāna. What, however, was my own ill—that I knew, and yet I went that road.

"That is one thing. The other is this. I was not straightforward with you when you were quite straightforward with me and trusted everything to our friendship. I ought to have informed you of this concealed idea of mine. And so it is I that am to blame for everything, and on me appropriately the punishment falls. Gladly, too, will I take it all upon me, if I could only know that no disturbance in your relationship has taken place through my rascally cunning. If anything of that kind should occur, Nanda, I do not know how I could bear it. If I have ever been anything to you, believe me this once when I say, 'She is the noblest, most intelligent, gentlest and faithfullest of all women.' That shall be the last cry that shall go forth from me into the world. My heart shall henceforth bleed behind the walls of the cloister; that shall be my punishment. You shall see me no more, save in the yellow robe and with shaven head. Cursed be vanity!

"You will say, 'What sort of punishment is that? For long already you have been living the life of a monk.' This is the punishment, Nanda; that I shall take with me, into the quiet of the cloister, a worldly heart, and that I shall take up the struggle against sensuality without any hope. And yet, in spite of all, something lives in me which calls me to further effort. I still retain an appreciation of the inestimable value of man's life. Wholly unhappy he only is, who has lost all faith in himself. This, indeed, is our blessedness, that, not only the evil, but also the smallest good bears its due fruit. The earnest may well again upraise a ladder of cobwebs out of the depths of their misery. To struggle here is to be victorious.

"But enough! I scent pride. Faults are to be quelled as long as they are at their beginnings.

"I have nothing more to say. I wish thee a true farewell, thou good, thou faithful one! O Nanda, forgive me!"

Punna to Nanda.

"Colombo, 24th November.

"A madwoman has been writing to you. To-day, one who has awaked from madness to reason writes to you.

"Nanda, I will tell you all, as frankly as I would tell it to myself. First of all, then, you must understand that I am to blame for everything. My pride, my foolishness have brought me to this pass, and plunged all three of us into misery.

"When I saw what a contemner of love this Kosiya was, I thought I would convert him and teach him the might of love. Wretch that I was! So I began a wicked piece of sport with him who first came under my roof as your friend. The more I saw how cold he was, the warmer did I become. You must understand, my—Forgive me! I cannot any longer so address you! You must understand that very soon I no longer sought to convince him through reasoning, but only through myself, just as if that were my highest duty, when, in fact, there was no higher duty for me, but to be devoted wholly to thee in love and esteem. The position of a betrothed is with us what the marriage state is among others. But I thought, 'Oh, it is only a piece of sport, which it lies in my power to give up at any time I choose. Besides, what harm can come of it to me? What to him? What to thee?' So our foolishness thinks.

"When I saw that I was not making any headway, I had recourse to cunning. I feigned illness and denied myself to him. I do not know how I fell into this—I who have always been a friend of straightforwardness. But surely it must have been my fate, else would the consequences not have been so terrible. I swear to you, however, that up till then I had never been anything but the actress.

"One day there was a knock at the door at an unusual hour. The servant was not at home. I opened the door myself. How I started to find Kosiya himself before me! I think I grew pale a little with surprise. As I looked at him, I noticed something peculiar in his glance, a sort of glow such as up till then I had never before seen in him. Suddenly I knew that he loved me, and with that the torture in my heart began. For no one can be quite insensible in face of the love of another. Also, I felt the weight of my guilt, and to-day it is inconceivable to me, why I did not make clear to myself beforehand all the consequences of my possible victory. There now began in me such a confusion of my feelings as I have never experienced at any other time in my life. Everything in me became vague and doubtful. My feelings towards him were different from those towards other men, but I could not tell whether I loved him, or whether I only thought myself pledged to him on account of my guilt. Heavens, how I speak! Thou wast indeed still present, but in so monstrous a fashion that I no longer knew even if I loved thee. Thus terribly was I punished for my wicked trifling.

"So I lived in a state of twilight gloom. O Nanda, what torture! This struggle for clearness! And those nights! When I look back now on those days, I know that I have fully atoned, and if I find any comfort at this present moment, it is in the thought, 'I have atoned.' For, how can one who has done evil find any peace except in expiation!

"I felt that I could now no longer perjure myself. It would have been useless, and would only have made both of us still more distracted. We were now together oftener than ever. I sat there like one justified, and spoke like a fool. He could not help noticing it and taking confusion for love. My inward struggles, on the other hand, only increased my confusion, and hence the possibility of illusion on his part. It seemed to me almost unthinkable, that there should have been a time when I was master, and could decide whether all these perplexities should or should not arise. Oh, if only we paid more heed to the beginnings of things, how powerful, how happy, how peaceful we all might be!

"So I carried on my jest with him, at first designedly, and latterly without design. I say, 'jest.' Oh, if it had only been clear to myself at least whether it was jest or earnest! As surely as I hope one day to be a better woman than I now am, I tested myself until I was utterly exhausted, tested myself with the utmost strictness, but I never attained to clearness in my mind. Nay, it seemed to me as if the more I examined myself, the more confused did everything become.

"I saw how he was suffering. I admired him that, in spite of all, he preserved his dignity and good manners, his sense of duty and his love to you. Then, the evening before yesterday, it all broke loose. I tell you this because I know that he himself will tell you. I felt that it must come. We would both have been overcome in the oppressive atmosphere. But when it came, it appeared to me to be so uncalled for, so outrageous, so like a hurricane. I have never in all my life seen a man in such a state of suppressed passion. I shrank; I was really frightened. Like a rude creature I only screamed out to him, 'Never! Never!' and fled into the house to my mother.

"Of the night that followed I cannot write you anything. I can only say that I finally came to a crowning height of pain where I felt, 'This is the summit. There is nothing beyond.' I was on the verge of madness. It was like a miracle. Suddenly I felt an irresistible craving for reflection, and at the same moment also I felt in myself the ability to reflect. And so I began to reflect, and, the more I reflected, the more peaceful I became. And, the more peaceful I became, all the more clearly I began to understand. I understood the origin of the relations between Kosiya and myself to lie in my foolishness and heedlessness. I understood that I did not love him, but only the high thoughts that had a dwelling-place in him.

"When I was quite clear about this, I began to reflect, 'What, then, is the origin of my love for Nanda?' It is noteworthy that the moment I put this question to myself, I was perfectly clear as to what its consequences would be. I saw in visible form the worm that gnawed at the root of our love. But I remained quite calm. It was a delight to me to go on further, step by step. It was a delight to me to bring clearly before my own eyes the uncertainty, the frailty, the misery of love. It seemed to me as if all at once I enjoyed the fruit of Kosiya's teaching. I was so full of peace that even the thought, 'I am the hateful instrument by which he himself may come at the fruit of the teaching' had no power to disturb my serenity.

"One thing I now know for a surety. No happiness in this world, not even the highest, can outweigh the torments which

I have come through during these last few weeks. It is clear to me now that, so long as I love, I am exposed to the possibility of these torments. This bare possibility frightens me. I ask myself, 'How shall I find shelter from this possibility?' Judge yourself. Is there any other way but this—wholly and completely to give up love? Ah, my good friend, I am so sad when I think upon you, but it is to me as if I had thought all love away, as the fire burns away the hedge. More clearly than I ever knew anything before in my life, I now know this. I cannot belong to you any more than to any one else. I am resolved to follow the straight road of peace and safety. Before you come back from Madras, both my mother and myself will have entered the cloister. To be sure, my mother says that a life of safety may be led in the house also. But why give chance more food to feed on than is necessary, in order to toy with our frailty? My mind is firmly made up, and so farewell! Ah, thou, my beloved, what suffering I have brought thee! How evilly have I repaid thy trust, thy faithfulness, unworthy that I am! If only you saw the tears that now roll down my cheeks, surely you would feel, not anger, but compassion! But do not think that anything whatever can make me weaken in my resolve. I go, not out of despair, but only because I have perceived something better than love, a happiness higher far!

"And so farewell!

"PUNNA."

Nanda received these two letters at the same time, and read them in the above order, because he considered that Kosiya's would be the more important and Punna's the pleasanter. When he had finished Punna's letter, he sat for a while as if stupefied, staring straight before him; then he laughed aloud as people laugh when they are mad, and then with closed fists began to belabour himself with all his strength on breast, face and head. At the same time he shrieked out wildly. "How spendidly you have carried it all out, O Kosiya! The bride lost! The friend lost! And the test of their faithfulness? How is it with that? Are they, then, true now?" He shrieked louder and louder, all the while beating himself more furiously with his fists. He would perhaps have killed himself if he had not fallen down fainting with exhaustion.

When he came to himself again, he dragged himself like a sick dog to the place where both the letters lay. Again he began to read them, but at first, like a drunken man, without apprehending their meaning. Then, little by little, things grew clearer to him. Here and there as he perused them, he nodded thoughtfully. When he had read through everything for the third time, he said quietly, "It seems to me that, when man puts questions to Fate, he not only frames the question but also the answer. I put a question to Fate out of pure wantonness, out of bravado. Is it not a trick worthy of admiration that, simultaneously with the beginning of the answer, there is present also the necessity of the answer? And the further the answer proceeds, all the more apparent becomes this necessity. And now this solution! So does Nature answer. She answers questions by the dissolution of what is questioned, perhaps also by the dissolution of the questioner."

Again he began to read. Suddenly he started.

"How was that, then?" He took up the other letter and read. Again he nodded thoughtfully. "Something peculiar in his glance; a peculiar gleam was in her eye," he murmured. "So a sudden flaring up has decided the fate of my love, that is, has decided my fate. But if each had only seen in the eye of the other nothing more than a mere reflection, and had taken that for something belonging to the other? Perhaps, if just at the moment of the opening of the door, a shadow had passed over Punna's or Kosiya's face, or a grain of dust had flown into the eye of one of them, or perhaps if the sun had been in another position—who knows? Can Punna be right about the frailty and the misery of love? I will think about it."

THE LOVE OF HUMANITY

CLOSE to the town of Colombo there lies a village named Mutwalla, inhabited for the most part by fishermen only, who live in plain mud huts; of fine-looking buildings there are but few. Hence it was nothing surprising that Revata's house, though certainly no palace, was yet the finest in the village. A neat veranda of dark wood, communicating with a staircase, ran round it on all sides; and a wide door that stood open all day provided passers-by with a glimpse of its comfortably furnished interior.

Revata's wife had died young, and he had scorned to marry again, notwithstanding the two children, a boy and a girl, whom she had left behind. Yet it was not that he had deliberately nursed his life long the wound which the parting from his wife had made in his heart, although he had loved her sincerely and had heartily esteemed her; for, if she had not been beautiful of feature, she had at least been gentle, kind and firm withal.

"A peaceable wife is the prettiest wife," Revata's mother had been accustomed to say. "Peaceableness, my son, is like daily bread; outward beauty and wit, however, are like seasoning. Marriage is a lifelong affair. A man in the long run can manage fairly well without seasoning, but he cannot manage without bread. Where there is peaceableness, my son, there is health; where there is health there is beauty."

How true his mother's words had been! How happily he had passed the few years of his wedded life with the wife of his choice! Cheerful but not boisterous, nicely but not extravagantly dressed, reserved but not bashful—such his wife had always been. Certainly his pain at her death had been great, but since on his part he had always been a good husband to her, always considerate, always kind, entirely devoted to her without any kind of reserve, the wound in his heart had healed in the natural course of time. For grief on account of the dead endures lifelong only where one has to say, "Too late! alas! too late!" It endures only where conscience tears off again and ever again the skin that has formed anew upon the wound.

And so Revata might well have entered again the state of matrimony but that he began to reflect, "Why *should* I again take a wife?"

And, while he was reflecting upon marriage, marriage passed him by.

His friends said, "Get married, Revata! It is the natural thing."

"What an extraordinary way of talking, this 'It is the natural thing!'" thought Revata. "It is like a screen behind which one may hide anything. It is like a mantle which one may draw over everything. Are we obliged to do a thing just because it is natural? It is also natural that each man should crush other men to the earth so as to make a roomier road for himself, like the elephant that tramples down the bamboo shoots in his path. We must ask, not what is natural, but what is good. What is 'good,' however—this has been clearly taught only by the Buddha, the Exalted One, the first among gods and men. 'Good' is not the doing of this or of that, for, what is called 'doing good' here is called 'doing bad' there. To the thoughtful man there is only one good: renunciation, giving up, letting go.

"What impels us to marriage? Sensuality. That, later on, the sensuality departs, and the care of a family invests us with an air of dignity—this certainly is no merit of ours. No one ever married solely that he might participate in the dignity that attaches to the father of a family. It is a good thing to resist sensuality."

So the years passed over the head of the reflective man. His reflectiveness, however, did not prevent him from clinging with the tenderest love to his two children, or from doing everything necessary for their proper upbringing. The boy was called Silananda, after his uncle, who was abbot of the neighbouring monastery. The girl's name was Amba, which means mango-fruit. She received her name in the following circumstances :—

Some time before the baby girl was born, it was the time of the year when mangoes are first ripe, and the mother was passionately fond of the fruit. One day a particularly fine mango fell to the ground. A maidservant spied it, and with the intention of giving her mistress a treat, burst into her bedroom (it was about mid-day) with the words : "See, mistress ! Look at this beautiful mango !" Contrary to her custom, however, the mistress was asleep. Waking with a start, she jumped up hurriedly from her couch. Very soon after this incident, the child was born, and it received the name of Amba. The boy was born about two years later.

At an extremely early age the latter exhibited signs of his father's inquiring, meditative spirit. The girl, on the other hand, seemed to inherit the peaceful serenity of her mother. She would sit perfectly still in the shade of the mango tree for hours on end. When her father asked, "What are you doing, my child?" she would answer, "Father, I am enjoying myself." "With what are you enjoying yourself?" "With what? Why, father, I am just enjoying myself." "My daughter, long may you retain such joy! It is the only kind of joy that leaves no bitter after-taste."

The father sent his boy to the leading Buddhist school in Colombo. He did not like Englishmen's schools. "They make streets and railways, and do all sorts of wonderful things which make the country rich, but when all is said and done, they only make us rich in wants, and leave us poor in contentment. The man of understanding will keep away."

His son, it must be said, was of another opinion. The older the boy grew, the more his leaning towards things European showed itself. The meditative character of Buddhism—the meditation that teaches the dissolution of one's self in one's self, went against his nature. The exact sciences were his delight; expertness therein his admiration.

When he had completed his studies at the Buddhist school at Colombo, he asked his father to send him to the High School at Calcutta.

Nothing could have been more distasteful to the father than this. He would very much rather have seen his son enter the Order of the Buddha, and apply his abilities in that direction, but he did not consider himself justified in disappointing a wish, in itself quite proper, and which his means amply permitted him to gratify. More than any other people, Buddhists regard their children merely as goods lent. So he gave his child the necessary equipment, and the lad sailed gaily away for Calcutta.

The youth was absent for four years. One day his father received a letter to the effect that the curriculum was drawing to a close, but that he considered it necessary, before returning home, to inform his father that he had been converted to Christianity.

He begged him to send a reply to this before he returned.

The father replied—

"Beloved son! It matters little whether a man calls himself Buddhist or Christian or by any other name. It does matter, however, that a man should be contented and at peace with himself. There is nothing better than this. If you think that the god of the Christians offers you more than the word of the Tathāgata,* well and good! I do not know this god, and see no necessity for learning to know him; for, in the Dhamma,† I clearly behold the conclusion of the whole matter. I think, however, that this religion, too, cannot do other than teach men to do good, to speak good and to will good. You cannot yet have so completely forgotten the religion of your childhood's days, as not to know that your deed stands closer to you than aught else in the world. Your deed is the mother's womb that has borne you; your deeds are the sons whom you beget. In the one thing, 'Be good!' all religions

* The Buddha. † Buddhism.

agree. To be frank, however, no religion in my opinion shows the way to being good more clearly than does ours. Therefore I am sad and anxious about you, but my love for you remains unchanged."

The son read this letter, not without mingled emotions. When any one goes over to another faith, he is prepared to do battle for his new faith and play the martyr. Both anticipations were nullified by what Nalanda called his father's indifference. His father made it all unexpectedly easy for him.

When his term expired, he returned home provided with letters to the clergy of the place. In Calcutta the idea had been impressed upon him that the noblest of all tasks was to work for the progress and elevation of the people, that the Indian people more than any other stood in need of this elevation, and that among them the task was simpler than elsewhere, since here, with the extension of Christianity, everything, or at least the greater part of the rough work, was already done. Such ideas are the glittering net in which youthful minds are caught.

Silananda had now lived for about a year in his father's house, and all his efforts were directed only to one end, he burned for one thing only—the elevation of his people, their diversion into the path of true culture, of progress, humanity, Christianity. Since his mind was completely filled with these thoughts, it was only natural that, every time it encountered a resisting object, something of its contents overflowed, and that little by little, despite his father's striking tolerance, a coolness sprang up between them. Revata disapproved of his son's activity. Religion to him was the highest good, but the highest good to him was something which a man should guard like a precious jewel, not put on exhibition at every street corner. And the highest religion to him was that religion which teaches one to treat the convictions of others with consideration and in a respectful spirit. Hence the Christian mission, which in its zeal swept over the old like some coarse broom, was in his eyes a despicable thing, and his son's activity on behalf of this mission an abomination. But he contained himself in patience with the thought, "His deed has nothing to do with me; it concerns himself more than any one."

One day towards sunset the two men were sitting on the veranda in front of the house in comfortable long chairs; the old man, a powerful-looking form just a trifle inclined to corpulence, the strong face framed in a short grey beard; the son, slim, neatly built, with big, living eyes. In accordance with Sinhalese custom the old man wore only a loin cloth, and on his bare feet, heavy leather sandals. The upper half of his body was entirely nude, and his head, with its closely cropped hair, uncovered. The son was dressed after the European fashion in a suit of light flannels, with immaculate linen and shoes to match.

The old man sat in thoughtful mood, occupied only with chewing betel. The young man, on his part, was busily engaged in studying a London paper which the Rev. Mr. Stevenson had given him earlier in the day.

He read the journal through from the first to the last word. Not only did the scientific, political and industrial news interest him; even the advertisements did not remain unread. Many of them told of such wonderful things, awakened in him such unaccustomed imaginings. Why! What a country that must be! How infinitely advanced in culture! Could his Ceylon, his Sinhalese fellow countrymen, ever be raised to such a height? It seemed to him as if he must jump up and act; do something, no matter what. His glance fell upon the lowered eyes of his father sitting there chewing betel, and, passing thence through the crown of the coco-nut palms which swayed majestically in the monsoon wind, rested upon the sea with its great snow-white surges. He appeared to have no eyes for the beauty, the sweet restfulness of his surroundings. The sun was on the point of disappearing there, far away over the sea. The evening sky glowed with unwonted splendour, until the mass of glowing colour extended high up into the zenith. Like a bath of coolness the sea wind passed over the limbs. Flowers exhaled their odour all around. Pretty little children were playing on the streets. Little things with nothing on but a string tied round their loins crawled about in the sand. In the middle of the road a brown little fellow sat in a wash-tub, and, under the supervision of his father who squatted on his heels in front of him, with comical gravity poured floods of water over his streaming little head. Laughing women went to the well with their water-pots, and men stood about the beach working over their nets and chatting the while.

For some time Silananda looked into the distance, then, as if bored, his eyes turned back to the paper. He had already reached the last page of this many-sided monster. He now read—

"Cut and combed hair bought by Madame X. . . ."

Those white people! How striking! What a perspective!

And further on he read—

"A high-minded, well-educated lady, young in years, desires to enter into correspondence with an equally high-minded and well-educated gentleman, with a view eventually to marriage in order to escape melancholy."

He read this a second and a third time, and then fell to reflecting.

Naturally of keen understanding and far superior in education and learning to the average European, he lost the faculty of criticism when confronted by this new world. He did not clearly comprehend this "to escape melancholy;" he was still too whole and healthy; but it met him like the piquant odour of some unknown dish, and marvelling much, he thought—

"What a world! What a life for a woman! It would be worth while, united with such a woman, to work by her side, to endeavour to help to ameliorate things."

Again he fell to reflecting. Turning suddenly to his father, he began—

"When I was on my way back from Calcutta, at Tanjore railway station, a sort of peasant came in, carrying nothing but his stick, and behind him came his wife, quite young, carrying on her hips a baby, and on her back the whole of the family travelling baggage as high as a tower. I tell you, father, as she came into the shadow of the hall, the poor woman was nearly dropping, yet she fondled the child, and without hesitation offered it to suck of her dried-up breast. The man stood by as if it were all none of his business. It was revolting. I went over to him and said in Tamil, 'The poor woman is very tired.' He didn't answer me. I went on, 'You mustn't burden your wife so much.' Then he replied calmly, 'It is her business!' At that I lost patience and I shouted at him, 'Man! brute! Is that the way to treat one's wife?'"

The elder man had listened to all this with composure. He had been annoyed, as he always was, when his son had begun to read the journal. The daily press in his eyes was the most pernicious of poisons, and most offensive in itself.

He now interrupted his son with the question—

"Are you quite sure that it was his wife?"

"Why, father! Who else could she have been? Besides, it certainly made no difference in this case whether she was his wife or simply a woman."

"You are quite right. But in what way did you make matters better?"

"Make matters better? What do you mean? I did my duty!"

"Do you really mean to say that you consider it your duty to call a stranger, a brute?"

The son got up hastily from his comfortable chair.

"Father, is it quite impossible to talk to you about such matters? Do you not see——"

"All right, all right, my son!" broke in Revata. "My question was merely a rather unfortunate joke. But, all jesting aside, I want to ask you quietly if you think that, by your interference in this affair, as to the upshot of which I am not in the least curious——"

Here the son interrupted him. "I will tell you the ending. This brute in human shape gave the poor woman a push and drove her to the other end of the hall. Revolting, I say! The authorities ought to have interfered."

"The authorities are the guardians of the State; they are not the guardians of morality."

"Cattle are treated with more mercy than human beings."

"My child, men are treated most mercilessly of all by themselves. Grow older, and you will understand that. But once more, I would seriously ask you, 'Do you think you did any kind of good to any one whatsoever by your interference in this affair?'"

Silananda hesitated. The elder man went on.

"You interfered in order to teach the man; you only succeeded in making him obstinate. Further, you interfered in order to help the woman; instead of help she received cuffs and blows. You were the third party in the affair; your heart was roused to vexation and anger. In other words, you hurt yourself, and you called 'Brute!' a man, who certainly acted without evil intent, and merely lacked better teaching. But, worst of all, you caused him to pass from unintentional to intentional harshness. Certainly the whole business had only one result—you offended your fellow man."

Silananda laughed scornfully. "So the other man did quite a meritorious action when he thumped the poor woman in the ribs?"

"Son! I ask you in all earnestness, 'What have you to do with others?' See to yourself! Struggle for yourself! You have made a mistake. In what way does it help you that another has made a greater? When you are hungry, does it appease your hunger to learn that another is still more hungry than you? If only people wouldn't be so ready to forget their own weal with thinking of the weal of others! The world as a whole would be far better off!"

"And now, father, I must tell you also, in all earnestness, that my faith teaches me that the supreme duty is to do good to others, to sacrifice one's self for others, to forget one's self in thinking of others. Love is the greatest of all things."

"Son! In the fabric of the world there is nothing so dangerous, so two-edged, so liable to misuse, as that same word, 'love.' Woe to the religion that is founded upon love! It rests upon a quicksand; it builds upon a rainbow. Love is a thing like the plantain stalk, which looks as if one might carve a stout staff or crutch out of it. When, however, you start upon your task, you find nothing but a rolled-up sheath, and your labour comes to naught. You get nothing for your labour but your labour."

"Do you then know of a tree that can provide a better staff or crutch?"

"Knowledge, my son! Not that knowledge, however, which is so termed by the world, but the knowlege which the Buddha has taught us: that all things are transient, that all things are painful, that all things are soulless. That penetrates to our innermost; that gives strength and support."

"I am very well acquainted with these formulas, but they have always appeared to me to be a poor guide for the world."

"Because you only learned them; never lived them!"

"Now, father, if everybody were to think like you Buddhists, if everybody were to care only for himself, what would become of the world? How would it ever make progress? Our very highest duty is to contribute our share towards the upward tendency, the evolutionary movement which we find in the world to-day."

The old man spat out his betel hastily.

"Do you really think so? I consider that the highest duty of every one is to see that the world advances in virtue and moral knowledge. If any one thinks to attain this by taking care for the world—well and good! Let him try! I should have thought, however, that, when one aims at an unknown goal, he ought to take the sure road. The sure road begins at the personal *I*. Let each man start there, and he will make the world better. Let each man take care to be good, and in so doing he will best take care for the world."

The son contented himself with a somewhat contemptuous smile. The elder man proceeded—

"I see well in what a net you have been caught. Here, the further one presses forward, the more completely does one become involved. Here yielding alone leads to victory. Do you really believe that there is such a thing as a continuous development of the world? You all take your shop-keeping tricks and technical juggling for development, and never think that true development does not lie outwards in the distance, but is an entirely inward affair. The heights of true development are to be found in the Buddha-thought. Than the knowledge which leads to the loftiest morality, and in thought to the annulment of self—than this, there is nothing loftier."

"If everybody looked upon it as loftiest to annul himself by thought, it would be a poor look-out for the world."

"Your foolishness betrays itself. Rather

we should have that age of gold of which the ancients fable. But don't distress yourself. They are but few who regard it as the loftiest to turn the searchlight of their thought inwards, and, in the accumulated illumination of the resulting cognition, to learn to know themselves. So that everything will continue to go splendidly, at least so far as that world about which you are so anxious is concerned."

"Then you think that in no way can one be of greater service to the world than by taking heed to one's own excellence?"

"One's own excellence is not a thing over which to take a comfortable nap. One's own excellence is a thing for which one must persistently struggle and fight, and when once a man really asks himself, 'How stands it with me?' and has really found out, 'It stands but ill,' and earnestly labours for betterment, then he must wrestle till the perspiration breaks from every pore in his body, like one endeavouring to extricate himself from a creeper-grown morass. And as such a one will look neither to the right nor to the left, but only to his own deliverance, so also will you look neither to right nor to left, once you too have recognised, 'So stands it with me!' and the question, 'What will become of the world?' will seem to you, of all questions, the idlest."

"Never, father! Activity in the service of humanity will always be to me the highest duty and the highest reward. Perhaps events will yet convince you that my manner of looking at things is superior to your passivity, by which, ultimately, everything is left just as it is; to mere stagnation."

"You are still young, my son."

At this moment Silananda's sister appeared outside.

"Father, there is a man out here. He wants a subscription for the Mission."

"Give him something. You know quite well."

The girl disappeared. Silananda stood reflecting for a moment. There came over him something like admiration for his father, because he adhered with such inflexible consistency to the precept that enjoins giving.

The next moment, however, he experienced something very much like annoyance at his own admiration.

"So that is how it is with your giving, father! You give, although in your heart you are opposed to the Mission and its work. You give, only that you may not fail to carry out the Buddha's precept. You give without love, and yet it is love alone that imparts value to any gift."

"You are hard on your father," replied the old man. He read his son's heart. "I give according to my means, because I have been taught to give. You are quite right; I gave just now without love; merely in order to do a meritorious deed, to do a good turn to myself; for giving is the easiest way to acquire merit. When, in proportion to my means, I so give, it does not concern me to whom or for what I give. If you really believe that love is the most important thing in giving, then you will only give for things which in your opinion are good. But where are we to find the standard test of what is good and what is evil? How can you know that you are not doing merely apparent good, or perhaps supporting an evil thing; or if, in giving to one man, you are not neglecting a more deserving man, or one in greater need of assistance; perhaps even letting him perish? So soon as you depart from the *I*, you are like a ship at sea without a compass."

He paused for a moment and resumed.

"To be sure, I am not exactly in love with the Mission, but that is only because I have not yet reached that height to which the Exalted One points the way. Had I reached that eminence, it would be impossible for me to cherish an unloving thought towards anything whatsoever in the world."

"But not a loving thought either."

"You are hard on your father," said the old man once more, but this time without smiling.

The son preserved an oppressed silence, and in a little while departed with the uncomfortable sensation of having wounded the father who had always manifested toward him the utmost care and love.

His way led to the Rev. Mr. Stevenson's,

who had invited him to call and see him in the evening.

About this time several important matters were on foot at the Mission. Only a short time before, a sort of colony of Christian converts had been established in the Kelani district, so as to withdraw them more effectively from old influences. Hitherto these people had lived in their huts and had only been visited by missionaries from Colombo. Mr. Cook, a rich merchant in the suburb of Colpetty, had promised a certain sum to be spent in the erecting a building in the European style, thus giving the whole affair the character of an institution, and Mr. Stevenson, the president of the Mission, had selected Silananda to be the leader of this particular project.

When the young Sinhalese arrived at the house, he was shown into the room where all the missionaries were assembled.

"My young friend," said Stevenson, addressing him, "we have unanimously agreed to select you as the head of the Kelani project. Are you prepared to take it up?"

"You know, reverend sir, that I am ready now and always to place all my energies at your service in this matter. I am burning with zeal."

"I know, I know," answered Stevenson. "To be quite frank, however, I must call your attention to the fact that we are scarcely prepared to give you any salary, at least to begin with."

"Upon my word," interrupted Silananda, "I would not have taken a salary had you offered it."

"Excellent, my young friend! But you have already heard that Mr. Cook proposes to expend a certain sum. A suitable house will be built, and something done for the poor who are denied all education. You see, there opens before you here a field of work, which under God's blessing will abundantly and more than abundantly repay all your efforts."

Silananda was silent with his tongue, but his answer gleamed from his eyes.

"At first," went on Stevenson, "you will travel out to the place every day and superintend affairs, teaching and exhorting. So soon as the house is all ready, you will take up your permanent residence there, so as to come into closer touch with your pupils. And so I bid you heartily welcome as our fellow labourer in the Lord's vineyard, and pray that God's richest blessing may descend upon our, and more especially upon your, labours."

He stretched out a welcoming hand to the young man, who seized it with the deepest emotion.

Mr. Ross, the secretary, a small, lean gentleman, now began.

"You must not think, young man—that is to say, I mean—we were not entirely unanimous with regard to you. Several other names were considered, that is to say, to be exact, one—the church-officer, Clark, who possesses the great recommendation of being a white man."

Stevenson grew uncomfortable. Silananda sat with his hands on his knees, feeling rather awkward, like a boy on certificate-giving day.

"That is to say," said Ross, after a glance

over at Stevenson, "not as if I meant to say that the colour of one's skin makes any real difference; on the contrary, your knowledge of the Sinhalese language and of Sinhalese ways and so forth is in your favour."

"As I have already told you, Clark drinks and is quite uneducated," Stevenson coldly interrupted.

"Quite so! No doubt he is open to some censure as regards that particular matter. That, in fact, was why we passed him over. But, er . . . you know your father——" He hesitated a little.

"My father is a man of honour."

"Certainly, certainly! Your father is a man of honour. No one doubts it. But you yourself know better than any one how much opposed he is to our work."

"I am old enough to be able to stand up for my own opinions."

"That is what we hoped, young man. It was for that reason that we resolved to entrust this more than usually responsible post to you. But to come at once to business. How old are you?"

"Twenty-five."

Ross noted it down.

"Born, where?"

"Mutwalla."

"Father and mother Sinhalese?"

"Yes," answered Silananda, somewhat surprised.

"Where were you educated?"

"But you all know this!"

"It is only in compliance with regulations, because we must send in a report about you," said Stevenson, with a rather forced smile.

"Your education, then?" Ross asked again, dipping his pen.

"At first at Ānanda College in Colombo; afterwards at the High School at Calcutta."

"Thank you! As soon as possible you will receive your formal letter of appointment. You are quite agreed, then, to work without any salary?"

"I have just said so."

"Good! Good!" Mr. Ross shut his minute-book.

"Gentlemen!" Mr. Stevenson now said in a loud voice, "I think we may now declare our sitting at an end," and, turning in a friendly way to Silananda, he said, "May I ask you to be my guest for this evening?"

Silananda looked his thanks.

The gentlemen all shook hands with one another and departed. When they had all gone, Stevenson turned to Silananda—

"Excuse me leaving you by yourself for a minute or so," and disappeared into the neighbouring room.

He had invited Silananda to be his guest this evening, solely because his kindly nature impelled him to make up as far as possible for the tactless behaviour of Mr. Ross.

Stevenson was a widower and had but one child, a daughter. It was only the previous day that the latter had arrived in Colombo by a German steamer, after a five years' stay in Europe. Stevenson did not exactly know what his daughter's views were with regard to race distinctions, and it only just now occurred to him that it might perhaps be a case of "out of the frying-pan into the fire," with his *protégé*. So he thought it advisable to give his daughter a few hints beforehand.

Silananda might, perhaps, have been pacing up and down the minister's study for two or three minutes, when the minister himself reappeared and beckoned him into the sitting-room.

Here, Henrietta Stevenson came towards him with a friendly smile, holding out her hand to him, and all three took their places at the tea-table which was already laid out.

Stevenson's daughter was too thin and her features too irregular for her to be called beautiful, but when she spoke or smiled, one saw nothing but the grey, expressive eyes, and the sweet curve of the mouth. The abundant, dark brown hair seemed only with difficulty to find room for itself on the well-shaped head, and looked to be almost too heavy for that slim, delicate neck to support.

"So you are Mr. Silananda. My father has told me what an unselfish warrior you are in the good cause. I am so glad to make your acquaintance. You see, I also have come here with the firm resolve to devote my whole life to this work. So I hope we shall in future work together."

Silananda was not quite ready with a suitable reply to this speech. The young lady proceeded rapidly—

"You have left Buddhism behind and have come over to Christianity. What a resolution! Especially since, in your case, no considerations of speedier promotion in the service of the State have entered into the matter. Any one who goes in quest of a new religion out of an inward necessity seems to me to be like one who lives his life twice over. It is magnificent! The moment when it is at last found must be divine!"

Silananda still kept silence. He felt almost oppressed by her words.

"You see," she went on, "I, too, have made investigations into all kinds of religions. Not that I have doubted our own religion or failed to find satisfaction in it. But it is the heart's travel-hunger, as it were, and the fatherland never seems more beautiful than when one returns to it from abroad. My fatherland is the word of our God, and at the end of all my religious pilgrimages I have returned to its bosom with a delight that has only been increased."

"Are not these somewhat daring, perhaps also unnecessary, experiments, Henrietta?" her father interposed. It could not be said that he had a weakness for studying the religions of other peoples.

"No, father! My faith is a natural, inborn thing that cannot be shaken by anything. My faith is so deep, that I am even prepared to appreciate the peculiar merits of other religions. For example, there is this Buddhism," she went on, again turning towards Silananda, "for one thing, the religion which, as an object of study, is surely the most interesting of them all."

"How so?" The two words came from him with shameful lightness. The interruption, however, appeared to her to be quite appropriate.

"How so?" she said with animation. "Why, because it is the only one of all the religions in the world which completely dismisses every idea of God, and which therefore is to be mastered purely with the understanding, through knowledge, without the co-operation of faith. There is something of the greatness, but also something of the coldness, of mathematics about this system."

"But Buddhism has hosts of gods."

"Yes, that is so, but they are only like so many supernumeraries upon the stage. The real hero of the drama is Kamma,* and Kamma, ultimately, is nothing but an idea which pertains to natural science put into a moral-religious form."

"Which idea do you mean?"

"I mean the idea of action and reaction. Every deed inevitably brings in its train its due consequence, as each stroke of the piston-rod inevitably produces the counter-stroke; as the body is always accompanied by its shadow. And just as the deed is, so also is the result. Hence, don't look to the right, don't look to the left! Look only at yourself and your deed. That is the morality of Buddhism in its entirety. It must be frightful to know one's self under such an iron rod. And just look at what follows! What

* Actions, both physical and mental.

frightful egoism! You must only never lose sight of the precious 'I.' But, as I have just said, the great thing in favour of this religion is that, without making use of faith, it leads its adherents to a definite conclusion. One cannot be taught to believe; one must be born with the capacity for it already present in one. Buddhism is the religion of the void of faith. Every inquiring, not indifferent, doubter is a born Buddhist."

"The Buddha's religion is the religion of all those for whom life is sorrow."

"That is the same thing, Mr. Silananda. Wherever there is no belief in God, one's whole life is an entirely aimless thing; something that had better not have been, therefore a painful thing."

"How deeply you have thought over these matters! Looking at things from this standpoint, do you consider the natural sphere of Buddhism to be an extensive one? I mean, do you consider that the percentage of unbelieving men in the world is a large one?"

"God be thanked, no! Else, what would be the use of our Mission in Asia? I believe that every mentally healthy person possesses tendencies towards faith, and that these tendencies only need to be directed into the right channels. No amount of instruction, no Mission, can make a man of faith out of a man void of faith. Conversion means no more than to change or modify faith."

She saw the admiration that spoke from his eyes. Flattered and roused, she went on with renewed vivacity—

"Just as a cork, no matter how deeply one pushes it down into the water, always comes up again, so a man void of faith, no matter how deeply he may be dipped in Christianity, will always be drawn back again into the sphere of Buddhism, and re-converted," she added, with conviction.

Dazzled, he did not immediately comprehend. Only, by her slight inclination in his direction, he knew that the last words contained something that applied particularly to himself.

Thus, one endowed with faith, however deeply he might dive into Buddhism, would still, by reason of his faith, always be forced out again, like the cork out of the water. Astonishing! He, for his part, had never represented to himself this peculiarity of the religion of his fathers in such clearly formulated fashion. Had this, then, been the effective cause of his own conversion? Was it this faculty of faith that had driven him out of Buddhism and into Christianity? Did he at all possess this natural faith? He had never yet tried to make all this clear to himself.

"You don't appear to agree with me quite," she again began. "It may be that I have misunderstood. Perhaps I shall have the opportunity of asking you many questions about these things; for some points are not yet quite clear to me."

"I shall very gladly place all my knowledge at your disposal; I only fear—you have already studied the matter so thoroughly—I am afraid I shall not be able to tell you anything more than you already know."

"Oh, you over-estimate my knowledge."

"It really seems to me, Henrietta," Mr. Stevenson again took the opportunity of interposing, "that you have already thought and read a good deal more about these things than is necessary. Do you remember that passage in Thomas à Kempis: 'What doth it profit us to know many and wonderful things concerning the which we shall not be asked at the Day of Judgment?'" With that he got up, laid aside the journal the pages of which he had been turning over during the conversation, and stepped out on to the veranda. He had scarcely got there when he called back into the room: "Mr. Cook is just going past. I know the livery. It looks very much as if he were going shooting again. At his time of life he ought to be more careful, and especially at this time of the year."

"But it is the cold season just now," said Henrietta.

It was, in fact, January.

"You do not appear to be so well informed about the climate of the country as you are about its religion. To be sure, the cold season is now on, but the along-shore wind is blowing, bringing fever and influenza."

Henrietta contented herself with smiling.

"Is Mr. Cook the gentleman who has placed at our disposal the money for the new building at Kelani?"

"Yes. And he is not a very rich man."

"How noble! I believe a girl might love a man for that reason alone."

"Only girls who have studied still more religions than you," said Stevenson, laughing. "In general, stature and a moustache weigh more in the eyes of marriageable maidens than any disposition toward philanthropy."

"I begin to doubt, father, if your knowledge of the human soul is a very deep one."

Henrietta's voice had an earnest ring.

"Do not misunderstand me, my child. I believe that nothing in the world is capable of such great sacrifices as a maiden's soul."

Henrietta did not appear to be quite satisfied with her father's reply.

"It is not here a question of sacrifice." She returned abruptly to Silananda, "How momentous the future must appear to you! I am so very glad that I am to work along with you. Just think what it will be when the house is ready and becomes a centre for the whole island. It is almost incredible what one can do even with very limited means, if only one does not lack persistence. Some years ago I was travelling in Germany——"

Silananda looked at her somewhat surprised.

"You must not think I am an heiress."

"Goodness knows, you are not," interrupted Stevenson with comical seriousness.

"But I am economical, have few wants, and can therefore do many things that richer people cannot do. Thus, in Berlin, I got to know an unmarried lady, insignificant to look at, but possessed of the rarest faith in God and of unequalled perseverance. This lady began by taking under her care some infants belonging to a deserted mother. She rented some rooms in a wretched part of the city and supported herself by begging, literally by begging, from day to day, with some help from two pious sisters. Little by little her labours extended. More children kept on coming, also older children. She rented the entire house without having in her possession the smallest reserve of funds; her only reserve was her faith in God. And now, on the site of the miserable hired barracks in which she began her work, there stands a noble building like a Gothic cathedral. Ah, it is so comforting to feel how much there is of divinity sleeping in mankind!"

"To me it also appears," Silananda here threw in, "as if our waking part were a common medium. The god and the devil, both sleep in each of us."

Miss Stevenson did not seem to pay much attention to this remark. She had spoken with increasing animation, and now was silent, her cheeks slightly flushed. She was evidently somewhat moved.

Stevenson, in the meantime, had taken up his journal again, and now held it out, opened, to his daughter.

"Look there, Henrietta! Some good pictures of Tamil women from Jaffna!"

Henrietta took the paper.

"How charming! Jaffna is in Southern India, isn't it?"

"Dear me! All your geography forgotten! Jaffna is in the northern part of our island."

"Oh, well, don't distress yourself about it, father. It won't be long before I know all that is necessary for me to know."

"Of that I have no doubt whatever," said Silananda, with conviction.

Miss Stevenson gave him a friendly look and turned again to the picture.

"These Indian women have something pleasant, something quiet, about them. I like them very much. The women of Europe—at least those of the upper classes—have something of an aggressive manner, and, what is worse, seem to regard it as their duty, as part of their charm, that they should possess this air of excitement."

"Permit me to ask the rather impertinent question, 'To which of these two classes do you consider yourself to belong?'"

"Oh, I! I like the Indian," she answered, with a coquettish look that gave the lie to her words.

"Then we are just as wise as we were

before," said Silananda, and then felt startled at his boldness. Her hearty laugh reassured him.

Stevenson said seriously, "God grant, my child, that you unite both in your person, so that you may rouse the indolent and calm the hasty."

He appeared to regard himself under obligations to give a different turn to the conversation. His daughter, however, did not seem disposed to allow the topic that had been raised to drop so soon. It was easy to see that it was one of her pet themes.

"I assure you," she went on, addressing herself exclusively to Silananda, "the European woman wants too much; she has been too much pampered. The men there have been saying to the women for centuries, 'We are your vassals!' And now, when they manifest an inclination to enter upon their dominion, they are astonished that the men contest it. It is all too stupid! They don't seem to know that they hold the overlordship only so long as they do not crave it."

"I thought the European women did not want lordship, but only equality."

"But just reflect! If woman retained her old position, and in addition obtained equal rights in public affairs, that would practically amount to lordship. It is only compensating justice that one should be lost where the other is attained. In my opinion woman should let her strength and her charm lie in her abandonment of all claim to lordship."

She looked at the young Sinhalese as if she expected an answer from him.

"Of course one must suppose that every man is capable of assuming command over his wife and his family. But, apart from such capacity, many a one, perhaps only too willingly, renounces the cares of such office."

She started, and a faint blush appeared upon her features.

"Yes, yes," she replied, somewhat confused. "So many threads run alongside one another in this modern woman question. It is so difficult to disentangle them all and do justice to every party."

"I consider womanhood in her present state of development the grandest product of modern culture," said Silananda, somewhat timidly.

She threw a suspicious glance at him. Was it then possible that a man in the twentieth century could speak such words without malign intent? But in those clear, brown eyes there lay no concealment. Really, India was still, after all, the old wonderland!

"You make it difficult for me to reply to your remarks. I will say this much, however, 'Woe to womanhood in its modern development, if it does not in all honour look beyond the horizon of marriage.' A woman who has become a reflecting being is in a bad way, if she has not learnt to see further than marriage."

Mr. Stevenson sat buried anew in his paper, and did not appear to be inclined to throw a fresh log upon the waning fire of conversation. Our Silananda felt a trifle dizzy. He was not prepared to give a deliberate reply. He had never had the opportunity of clearly thinking over this subject. There was a pause. The Tamil servant on the veranda outside was heard preparing for the night. Silananda remarked that it was time to go.

As Miss Stevenson gave him her hand in parting, she once again said—

"To our faithful copartnership!"

"Yes, to our faithful copartnership!"

How he came back the long way to Mutwalla, Silananda never knew. He was as one lifted up and borne along upon the breast of some mighty wave. He was quite astonished when he found himself in front of his father's door. He imagined he had but just left the clergyman's bungalow. What had happened? His life, so it seemed to him, had only begun this day. Everything up till this hour looked dull and meaningless.

"Dear God! Now to work; to work! Now to lift one's self high above—above whom? Above no one, above the common mass."

In his room there was again no light. At other times he would have scolded the servant about it; to-night he scarcely noticed it at all. He undressed in the dark. His face still glowed, his pulse still bounded, as he fell asleep.

The very next morning he received a letter from Mr. Ross, giving him more detailed instructions as to how he was to direct his activities in Kelani. He was to give exhortations, instruct the children, and, above all things, to see to it that the regulations already laid down were strictly observed.

This he found more difficult than he had anticipated. The people clung to old use and wont, and yet they were to be educated, and that in the shortest possible time, to new habits of living, new views of life. They were to eat, dress and sleep in another fashion, and to accustom themselves to orderliness and various devotional practices. Silananda was not well fitted for his office, for he lacked that most important of all virtues to a reformer in India—patience.

The first days were passed in perpetual embroilment. When he came home one evening from Kelani, after he had been about a week at his task, he found a note awaiting him from the Reverend Mr. Stevenson, requesting him to call at his house that same evening.

He started out immediately.

He found father and daughter in the sitting-room, engaged in a lively conversation.

"Only think," began Stevenson, "what a terrible misfortune. Mr. Cook is dead!"

"Good heavens, do you say so? I thought I saw him early this morning as I was on my way to Kelani."

"That is very likely. It was only this afternoon that he met with the accident. He was going out shooting, and a strong wind was blowing along the shore. He wanted to give some order to his driver, but did not want to shout to him. So he got up as his carriage was moving, and in sitting down again made a false movement, fell out, and his temple unfortunately struck on a sharp stone so that he was taken up for dead. Two hours later he died without once recovering consciousness. Serious fracture of the skull. How careful one ought to be. Yes, Mr. Cook is dead," Stevenson repeated, glancing at Silananda.

"Ah, now I comprehend!" Silananda cried. "How deplorable!"

"Precisely. You have said the word. We are all mortal men. Each of us must daily say to himself: 'This night thy soul shall be required of thee;' but this blow is no light one to us, because Mr. Cook had not yet completed his gift, and naturally has left nothing in writing behind him concerning it. All our plans have gone to the wind, perhaps for ever."

"For goodness' sake, don't say that, father!" his daughter cried in agitation.

"What does the sum amount to?" asked Silananda.

"Oh," said Stevenson, "there is not the slightest prospect of getting it. The merchants all complain of bad times. You know, this unfortunate war in South Africa has affected our trade also for the bad. No one can donate a large sum, and the few who might are indifferent."

"Might I ask you to let me know what is the sum required?"

Stevenson grew attentive. "It is not so very much; but, as I have already said, quite unattainable. Three thousand rupees at the very least. Moreover, the affair is already public. The land has been marked out, and materials arranged for. It is too bad altogether."

"Father," Henrietta cried, "let us do as that German lady did. Let us trust in God and begin with nothing."

"My child, that is easily said. I don't know whether beams and labour are to be had for nothing in Germany; but here they cost a lot of money. And where are we to get them? You see, our situation is quite different. We stand here in the open. Everybody is looking at us. And if our scheme fails, it is much worse than if it had never been undertaken. There is that Dharmaratna with his Buddhist journal at Pettah; there is that advocate Pereira. They will let out a shout of triumph. And then—you don't know all the circumstances here

—the Catholic Mission—they too will be jubilant. We are living in the world and have got to reckon with the world. Mr. Silananda understands more about it and will agree with me."

Silananda scarcely heard Stevenson's words, but stood lost in thought. When the clergyman had finished, he said—

"Perhaps I might be able to provide the money."

"Father in heaven!"

Henrietta stepped towards him. He saw how her breath came and went.

"To be sure," began Stevenson, "that would be——" he stopped.

"Pray explain yourself, Mr. Silananda!" cried Henrietta.

"A mere loan of the money would be entirely useless," Stevenson again began.

"I quite understand."

"Your father, of course, is a rich man."

"My father has only as much as permits him to live at his leisure, and would never be induced to give any donation to the

Mission. But there is our mother's legacy. It is certainly—I don't yet know, but I will see."

"My dear young friend," began Stevenson, "you know how highly I esteem you, and how kindly I mean it when I say to you, 'Ponder well over what you are doing.' You have entered into connection with us, so to speak, as our employee, who eventually, later on, will receive a salary from us, and now you transform yourself, so to say, into our benefactor. You are still so young," he added hesitatingly.

Our Silananda felt as if he had been struck in the face with a whip. "All that is now needed," he thought, "is that he should reproach me with my brown skin."

"Mr. Stevenson, do you not think me sufficiently honourable to help the Mission to the utmost of my power?"

"Oh, my dear friend, how you twist things! As God is my judge, I never had anything of the sort in my mind. You know well how much we have all built upon this idea, and if you should be in a position to provide the money—why, our thankfulness to you could scarcely be put into words."

"My father is right," interposed Henrietta.

"I will not at present promise too much, but I certainly think that I can raise the sum. At any rate, I give you my word of honour that I will do all I possibly can. I will let you know definitely to-morrow."

With that Silananda took his leave. In the street he knocked up against Mr. Ross.

"Have you heard," began the latter, "that Mr. Cook is dead, and that with him go all our plans?"

"I have just come from Mr. Stevenson's."

"You visit Mr. Stevenson very often."

"He had invited me."

"Oh, indeed! His daughter is quite upset."

Silananda had firmly made up his mind to let him know nothing of his offer, but now he answered, only that he might conceal his partial embarrassment—

"We have been considering how the money may still be obtained."

"Have you really?" cried Mr. Ross, in a

sarcastic voice. "You have already achieved important results?"

"I hope the thing can be done."

"You hope. Indeed! Then I must be off to Mr. Stevenson's immediately. The ways of Providence are often difficult to understand," he added irritably. "Good-bye! Good-bye!"

He hastily proffered him his hand, and at the same moment hailed a passing vehicle.

When Silananda came home he found his father and his sister sitting on the veranda. The night air was like balm; flashing fire-flies flew hither and thither; the sea-breeze murmured through the leaves of the trees.

The old gentleman, as ever, sat chewing betel. His daughter sat near him. Over her short silken jacket she had thrown a shawl which covered her shoulders. A white flower gleamed in her hair. In front of her lay the dainty embroidered slippers. She herself sat, her bare feet up off the floor, crouching upon the chair. One hand lay in her lap, the other hung loosely over the arm of her chair. She was gazing quietly into the night. She looked very sweet in her perfect modesty.

As her brother stepped on to the veranda, she let down her feet and slipped them into her slippers. She knew that he did not like to see her squatting "like a jungle woman."

"You are still up?"

"The night is long," replied the old man in an even voice. "Watching is better than sleeping."

The son sat down on a chair, but immediately got up again and restlessly began to walk up and down. The firm tread of his feet rang unpleasantly loud in the quiet night. This European unrest jarred on the old man. He held it more seemly and fitting to sit still. "The quieter the body, the more active the mind."

Amba knew what was passing in her father's mind concerning her brother's marching up and down. In the most unpremeditated way, she said—

"Do sit down, Sila! The night is so beautiful."

He mechanically obeyed. "Yes, you are right; it is a beautiful night."

"You have had important news from Mr. Stevenson?" she went on.

She saw that something lay upon his heart.

"Thank God!" he thought. "The question comes very opportunely for me."

"It is something about which I would like to talk with you."

The old man did not stir. Amba, however, said good-naturedly—

"Really, you are making us inquisitive, Sila."

"Yes, only think! Mr. Cook met with an accident and died this afternoon. You will remember that Mr. Cook was the gentleman who was going to give the money for the building in Kelani. Now everything is upset. Mr. Stevenson was very much shocked. All of us naturally the same. We talked it all over. To cut it short, I could not help myself; I have undertaken to provide the money."

The old man still maintained silence. He

sat there in the darkness like an immovable block.

"But how much is it?" asked Amba, with forced indifference.

"Oh, somewhere about two or three thousand rupees. You see, father," he turned to the old man, "I don't need to make so much ado about it; for I can dispose as I please of the two thousand rupees from our mother, since I am now of age——"

"Yes, my son."

There was something so peculiar in the tone of the old man, that Silananda became still more embarrassed and broke off.

"What does Miss Stevenson say about it?" asked Amba, innocently.

"Miss Stevenson! What should she say? Women in general have not much to say in such important matters."

He could have kicked himself as soon as he had said these words. He knew that both his father and his sister read his heart like an open book.

He had described the fair foreigner as a model of discretion, capable of governing men. He was acting like a schoolboy. It was unendurable. Everything in him rose in revolt. He proceeded almost insolently—

"But that has nothing to do with the present affair. In one word, father, I would ask you to give me another thousand to add to my two thousand. Of course it is understood that I will pay you back to the last farthing."

"How do you expect to be able to pay back?"

"How?" replied Silananda, somewhat irritated. "Well, I think if one works and is diligent, he won't be very long before he will be able to pay back a thousand rupees."

"Mere diligence and running around won't do it. Whoever runs after people finds that people keep out of his way."

"But all this, father, has nothing to do with the money."

"Quite correct, my son! Talk is always bad; so let me say at once: 'I will not give the money.'"

"I foresaw this possibility," said Silananda, somewhat precociously. "So I want to ask you to give me your permission to approach my sister about this loan."

"Your sister also is of age and has good sense. Amba has good sense. Ask her."

"I will give the money, father."

"It is all you have. You have made up your mind very quickly."

"I had already made up my mind."

"I only fear it will be a heavy blow to Sinha."

With that Revata left the veranda.

Silananda went over to his sister.

"Amba, how can I possibly thank you? How good you are!"

"Father is right. It will be a heavy blow to Sinha. I didn't think of that at all."

Sinha was the trader with whom their maternal portion had remained out at interest for quite a number of years.

"Oh, he does a big business. What do a thousand rupees matter to him?"

"It isn't one thousand, but three thousand rupees."

"Quite true; but even if it is three thousand, he won't miss them."

"Do you really think so? I shrink at the thought that I may be harming one, in order to do good to others. He has always paid his interest so promptly."

"Don't trouble about it, Amba! Leave it all to me. Do you know," he proceeded somewhat abruptly, "it is such a long time now since last we spoke peaceably to one another."

"Since you came back from Calcutta you have always had so little time."

"No, not quite that. But you do not now understand me so well. Your interests have become so different from mine."

"Sila, I am thinking that it is your interests, not mine, that have changed."

"Ah, Amba, if you would only allow yourself to be convinced! If only you would abandon your passivity! If only you would recognise the blessedness of labour, of effort for others! How unspeakably elevating it is to labour in the service of humanity, to give one's self in love to the whole human race! You have no idea what a position women are in for bringing out the best that is in their fellow men. You have a good understanding."

A smile stole over the girl's face. He did not see it. He went on eagerly—

"For you also there is plenty to do amongst us. The Christian religion has such wide, such loving arms."

"Don't trouble, Sila! I think it is also something to keep quietly to one's self and leave the world in peace."

"What do you mean by that, Amba?" There was something of irritation in his voice.

"In working for others it is so easy to forget one's self. But how can one attain salvation if, occupied with others, one forgets to work for one's own salvation?"

"Working for others is salvation."

"Working for others is only a method of binding ourselves ever more closely to life. But life is so full of suffering."

"What do you know about suffering, sister? You live in comfort and quiet, surrounded only by love."

"Is it not suffering to look upon transiency, upon the passing away of everything?"

"What ideas to have at your age! You are your father all over again!"

"The Buddha has taught me. Every one follows his own nature."

He would have liked to say something in opposition, but quite obviously he was determined for this day to treat his sister with tenderness.

"How old are you now, Amba?"

"Two years older than you, Sila."

"So you are already twenty-seven. It is getting to be high time that you were marrying. It is odd that I haven't thought more about that."

She smiled a little.

"How is it, Amba?"

He drew up to her confidentially. With perfect equanimity she replied—

"If it is my Kamma to get a husband, I am quite prepared. If it is my Kamma to remain single, I am quite prepared. My time is past. But you, Sila? It is getting to be high time for you also to be looking about you. Your schoolfellows already have children."

He put on a scornful look. Obviously he was in a haughty mood.

"Oh, they!" he said. "They take life in a different way from me. But I must be going now. What time is it?" He drew out his watch. "How annoying! With all the confusion of the day, I have forgotten to wind up my watch. I don't know how late it is now."

"You don't need a watch for that. Look at the Southern Cross. It must be about twelve o'clock."

"Off to bed with you, Amba; off to bed!"

* * * * *

Early next morning Silananda got ready to visit Sinha the trader. The latter lived in the Pettah, the Sinhalese quarter, near the big bazaar.

Silananda did not like going into the Pettah. The bustle and noise grated on him, and the peculiar heavy air, as if expressly perfumed, oppressed him.

He went on his way swiftly, without very much thought as to what he was going to say. Only when he had passed the bazaar did he begin to reflect upon his errand. Sinha's shop lay immediately behind it. Silananda stopped directly in front of a fruit stall, and stared at the heaped up coco-nuts.

"Fresh, cool coco-nuts, sir!" the seller called out to him. "Want to drink?" and he got ready to cut the top of a nut with his heavy knife.

Silananda turned away quickly. A few steps further on, and he had come to a stop again before another stall.

"Bombay mangoes, sir! or these bananas! Sweet as sugar!"

He pulled himself together and strode straight up to Sinha's shop.

Sinha was a dignified-looking gentleman, with a black beard and a tortoise-shell comb stuck in his long hair. He wore a European jacket and the loin-cloth of the Sinhalese.

As Silananda entered, Sinha looked at him in astonishment.

"Do my eyes deceive me? What an honour for my house! Mr. Silananda! What brings you here?"

In his surprise he had spoken in English, but he now turned quickly back to Sinhalese.

"Please take a seat, sir!" he said, and hastily wiped a footstool.

The young assistant in the shop, in his curiosity, forgot to pack up again the balls of cotton which he had just spread out before a purchaser.

Silananda seated himself, took off his hat, and wiped the perspiration from his brow.

"What an honour for me!" again said Sinha, and placed himself smiling before his guest.

"How oppressive it is to-day!"

"To-day!" cried Sinha. "But this is one of the cool months. You have been quite spoiled in Calcutta; quite spoiled." And he laughed as at a highly witty remark.

Silananda made an attempt to laugh with him. He felt extremely uncomfortable. What a disagreeable errand!

"How goes business, Sinha?" he asked lightly.

"Oh, we get our living out of it, but we have to be diligent and keep our eyes about us. You see, it is pretty hard to compete with these Bombay fellows. They get hold of every visitor down at the jetty and hardly anything comes our way. There they stand in front of their stalls like so many sharks with jaws wide open, and if one only lets his glance turn in their direction, down they come on him, crash through everything. I am not like that. When any one comes my way, I make my salaam and say politely, 'Fine goods here, sir. Step inside, sir!'"

"So Europeans also patronise you?"

"Why should you think so?"

"On account of your takings."

Sinha was taken aback.

"On account of my takings? They are pitiful enough. As I said, we manage to maintain ourselves."

"But you have a neat little house on Mount Lavinia."

"Oh, but just think, sir! Could I keep

the children here, four of them, to be stifled in this air, or to be trodden down in the streets, or come to see bad things?"

"Well, well; but they are not exactly princes!" And emboldened by his own rudeness, he proceeded valiantly: "I must ask you to let me have my two thousand rupees together with the thousand of my sister."

"Ye two and thirty gods!" cried Sinha. "Do you want to dash me to the ground? What have I done to you? Have I not paid you your interest year after year, in good times and in bad?"

"I know that, Sinha, and I thank you for it." The words had a studied ring about them. "But now I want the money itself."

"But how can you want it? Even when you went to Calcutta you didn't want any of it. How, then, can you want it now?"

"It is—I can't explain everything about it to you—it is on account of a bit of land I am buying."

"Land you are buying? Now? In times like these? Let me advise you——"

Silananda interrupted him.

"It is connected with an affair at Kelani."

A light broke upon the merchant.

"Now I understand. You are going to help feed the idle gluttons at Kelani."

"What has taken you, to speak like that about people who have had the courage, after due consideration, to choose a new religion; a religion," he added in an elevated voice, "to which I also belong?"

"Yes, I know. Your father came and told me of his sorrow at it. Excuse me for speaking so, but I am a simple man who can t hide what he feels. Sila," he went on, almost coaxingly, "I knew you when your mother was still carrying you in her arms. At that time you had just as big eyes and not such a big stomach as the other children. How often I said to your mother, 'What a child!' And I was glad when your mother was glad. Sila, think of my wife and my little children. Do you really mean to imperil my livelihood for the sake of these lazybones? Don't imagine that they have changed faiths out of conviction. The attraction has been the missionaries' rice and cotton."

He suddenly became aware that his tongue had run away with him again. He pulled himself in quickly.

"They may, perhaps, be good enough people—indeed, I have heard about one of them that he knows the whole Bible by heart, only he doesn't live in Kelani. But why not let the rich Christians look after these people? They are living on the fat of this poor land. They milk and milk and never think of what the Buddha says, 'Leave some milk in the udder!' Are we jackals, that we should snap at one another? Who will lend me another three thousand rupees, now, in these hard times? And if I can't get them I don't know what will become of me."

The perspiration stood on the young man's brow. With an effort he got out—

"But I must have the money."

"Could you not wait for a year?"

"Quite impossible!"

"Half a year? Do have a little mercy, sir."

Silananda could not stand it any longer.

"I will talk to them."

With that he seized his hat and rushed out. He strode blindly on and on, incapable of a single connected thought. What was he to do? How could he approach Stevenson?

Suddenly he heard some one calling his name. Collecting himself, he looked up, and found himself in front of one of the large shops in the neighbourhood of the harbour. Then he perceived that Miss Stevenson was addressing him. Only his brown skin concealed his sudden change of colour.

She appeared to be on the point of entering the shop. The rickshaw from which she had obviously just alighted stood in the street. The Stevensons had no carriage of their own.

"Mr. Silananda, you come like a messenger of Providence."

Puzzled, he looked at her. Quite evidently he experienced some difficulty in assuming the *rôle* of messenger of Providence at a moment's notice.

"You see," she proceeded briskly, "I was just on the point of going in here to get a lot of new things, when I saw you, and immediately the thought shot through my head, 'This is a token! Really one ought to be ashamed of one's self. Here I am on the point of squandering money, and out there the most difficult tasks are waiting to be done.' Here! Take it! It is fifteen pounds. I can still find at home a few summer clothes."

Thereupon, despite his resistance, she forced the money into his hand.

"Where were you going just now?"

"How ashamed of myself you make me, Miss Stevenson!"

"I make you ashamed of yourself? That is good. But I think we can never get too much money together."

Silananda experienced something of the torments of the damned.

"But what is the matter with you?" asked Miss Stevenson.

"I must see your father on urgent business."

"You will just catch him at home. We will go together."

Silananda hailed a coolie.

Just as Miss Stevenson was stepping into her rickshaw, she turned round and called to him—

"I forgot the most important thing of all. How is the affair progressing?"

She smiled confidingly at him. He was already seated in his vehicle, and, having made it come a little nearer to her, he said—

"I am just going to consult your father on that very matter."

She fixed her eye on him once more for an instant, then she mounted hastily, gave her address, and they both proceeded, one behind the other, towards the missionary's house.

As they stepped on to the veranda, Stevenson came towards them, all ready for going out.

"Look there now! You back already?

And Mr. Silananda, too! Good morning." Then, noticing the faces of both, he asked, "Has something happened?"

Henrietta turned away.

"Mr. Stevenson, I would like to have another talk with you about yesterday's affair."

Stevenson looked at him expectantly. "The trader with whom is lodged the money of which I spoke is, for the moment, not in a position to pay it. He asks for six months' grace."

"I can quite understand that," said Stevenson, smiling.

Silananda looked at him in a disconcerted fashion.

"Yes," Stevenson went on with a laugh, "who willingly gives up money?"

"So you mean—I thought——"

"But who is it?"

"A man called Sinha."

"Has a place near the bazaar? Deals in cotton, linen goods, etc.?"

"The very man."

"I can well believe that he *will* not give,

but I will never believe that he *cannot* give."

"He pictured to me the ruin that would overtake him if I withdrew the money immediately."

"That is hardly possible with such an extensive business. I assure you, these people would allow themselves to be flayed to death before they would loosen their purse-strings. It is really pitiful about these trader people in our big towns. They have no religion. They have lost their old religion, and they don't want the new. O God, if only Thou wouldst bestow Thy blessing, so that a remedy might be found!"

"You have really rolled a load off my mind. I was afraid of plunging the man into distress."

Henrietta now came in.

"But are you quite certain, father?"

"Child, I know the present circumstances better than you do. If we were to wait until a trader in the Pettah hands over anything—oh, it is comical merely to think of such a thing."

"I am quite certain that when I go to see him again, he will talk me round the very same way again."

Stevenson looked at him in a kindly, compassionate manner.

"My dear friend, it is certainly not our business to take money from people against their will; but really, I know your countrymen better than you do yourself. You know how cautiously I accepted your noble-hearted offer yesterday. You know that it was yourself who had to complain of not being considered worthy."

Silananda lowered his eyes. "But now, taking all the circumstances into consideration, just think! On the one hand, countless hundreds needing help—a work of humanity; on the other, a trader unwilling to pay up. Before God, I for one could not hesitate a moment."

"Certainly," said Henrietta softly, "it is one against so many." "So many!" she repeated meditatively.

"I am quite clear about it now. My mind is made up."

"Could we not assent to the respite of half a year?" asked Henrietta.

"Not at all, not at all," replied Silananda. "At the end of the half year he would have the very same story to tell."

"Apart from that," began Stevenson, "the thing is this: we are now in January. If we wish to build soon at all, building soon means building right on; for everything must be under cover before the beginning of the rainy season. Half a year from now, we shall be right in the middle of the rainy season. Hence, to wait for half a year simply means to put off the affair for a whole year. But what that means in its effect upon the entire undertaking I need scarcely set forth at length."

"Mr. Stevenson is right. We must fix a very short time as our limit, if the whole affair is to be carried out in a satisfactory manner. The only thing is, I don't quite know how I am to let the man know my final decision."

"Why, just write to him!"

"Could not Mr. Douglas, perhaps——?"

"Really, Henrietta," broke in Stevenson, "that is quite an idea. I'll tell you what. If we want to go about the affair quite securely, let us first of all consult my man of law, Mr. Douglas. He is an elderly, experienced man, and knows the circumstances very intimately; you can rely upon his advice. Indeed, he was here early this morning, and our conversation turned upon you."

Silananda could not conceal the feeling that he considered himself flattered.

"Certainly, that I will do," he said briskly.

"Perhaps you will allow Mr. Douglas to carry through the whole affair?" said Henrietta.

"Will Mr. Douglas, however, be willing to write the letter for me?" said Silananda, dubiously.

Miss Stevenson blushed, and the clergyman stared in unconcealed astonishment.

"You must, of course, pay him something," she said. "That is his profession."

"Oh, of course, of course. I forgot that. Where does Mr. Douglas live?"

"At the Cinnamon Gardens, on the sea-ward side, close to the German Consul's house. Any rickshaw coolie will take you there."

"Very good. I'll be off at once."

"By the way," Stevenson called after him, "all the necessary arrangements have already been made with the contractors. We could make a start to-morrow if the money were forthcoming. But you will see what Mr. Douglas says."

Mr. Douglas was an elderly gentleman with grey haïr and beard cut short. He had something of military brevity about him.

When Silananda gave his name, he said courteously—

"I heard about you early this morning from Mr. Stevenson."

Silananda laid his case frankly before him. He had a feeling of being at home, to some extent, in the company of these Englishmen. It was a sort of pleasure to him to show these men how thoroughly his mind was made up to deal firmly with Sinha. Besides, it was quite clear to him now that the latter was simply obstinate.

When he had finished, Mr. Douglas said—

"Will you please let me see the documents?"

"Which document?"

"At the time when the money was lent to Sinha, you must have received a form of receipt."

Happily he had the paper in his pocket. Mr. Douglas read it through.

"According to this, by our law, you can insist upon immediate payment. You can demand the money to-day, even."

Silananda had some difficulty in not revealing by a smile the pleasure he felt. It was really a wonderful thing, this modern civilisation and its various contrivances.

"You mean that without any trouble I can have immediate payment?"

"What trouble do you need to take to ask back your own money when you want it? Of course, he will never give it willingly. And," he added, with a quiet smile, "you don't know these natives—that is," he quickly corrected himself, "these indigenous traders. They would let themselves be tortured with pleasure, they will whine for mercy for God's sake, they will shed genuine tears, if only they can save their precious money. We know all about that, believe me, so you need not give yourself the least concern. I will do what is necessary immediately."

"When do you think I could be in possession of the money?"

"Ah, now, that is coming to the point," said Douglas, with cordiality. "In two days, at the very outside."

"Splendid!" thought Silananda.

He rose to go, for he observed that much talk was out of place here. With a shake of the hand he took his leave and went home.

The midday meal in his father's house was always eaten in silence. That was one of Revata's strict rules. "Heedfulness pertains to eating," he was accustomed to say. "In eating, one must constantly reflect that one does not eat for enjoyment, but only that one may nourish this body."

This paternal regulation suited the son very well this day. He feared unpleasant questions.

When the meal was finished, the mouth rinsed out, and the hands washed, Revata said—

"To-morrow will be the dedication of the new statue of the Buddha at Kandy. Your cousin Sabakami told me. We haven't been," he proceeded, turning to Amba—"we haven't been at that sacred spot for a long time now. I think we will set out to-morrow."

"Oh, that affair that is advertised in the *Colombo Times?*" said Silananda.

"In the newspaper?"

Amba sprang to his assistance. "Father, how else could the faithful learn about it? The more there are present, the more impressive it will be."

"Certainly, of course. They couldn't do anything else. What does it matter?" With that he rose up and went out of the room. In going he called to her, "Come along, then, Amba. We must get things ready."

The girl ran quickly up to her brother. "How is it with Sinha?"

"Everything is arranged, sister."

She slipped away after her father.

That evening Silananda came back late from Kelani, much later than usual. His father and his sister were already in bed. Next morning quite early both started on their journey. There was only a brief and quiet parting. The Buddhist is no friend of moving scenes. To him weeping and lamentation is ignorance. Silananda, on his part, was at heart rather glad at their going away.

His father had said nothing as to when they would return. "How can man be so lacking in reflectiveness as to say, 'To-morrow, or, in three days, or, in such and such a time, I will return home?' Can we say anything certain even about the next minute? Only fools would venture to do so. The wise man knows that our life is even as the ripe fruit upon the tree, which may be expected to fall at any and every moment. Yea, the wise man knows still more. He knows, 'There is no future.' That which we call the future only arises with my arising, only arises through me. How can I say anything about that which as yet is not?"

So thought Revata. So think all who have been taught by the Exalted One.

On the day after their departure our Silananda sat contentedly on the veranda. Not yet high noon, it was delightful to sit there in the cool shade. Sky and sea shone; the rustling of the coco-palms, the distant sea-surges, both sounded so soothingly.

He had in his hands a pamphlet by a certain Mr. Pereira. This man, of a name that indicated Portuguese extraction, was yet an enthusiastic Buddhist, had visited England, and there had studied for several years in a high school, and was now a practising advocate. He was a most zealous and capable defender of his faith against Christian intruders. For, it is not the case in Buddhism as it is in other religions, that the clergy are its protectors and supporters. The principal virtue of the Buddhist Monks consists in a deliberate passivity, in care for one's own salvation by striving towards Nibbāna; that is to say, by cultivating freedom from desires. Anything that is done here in defence of the religion of the country is done by the laity.

This Pereira had chosen as the subject of his pamphlet the theme, so well beloved, of a comparison between the two religions. In glowing colours he depicted the restraints which the religions of revelation had imposed upon healthy thought; the *sacrifizio dell' intelletto* which they required of every faithful believer. He painted the breach which had occurred between science and religion, which must of necessity go on widening, and which, in fact, in European lands was yawning ever deeper. He described in weighty words the means adopted in earlier times to put an end to this cleavage. He spoke of the Holy Roman Inquisition, and here the mocking tone of his language was terrible. He spoke of fanaticism and of its origin in these dogmas that gave the lie direct to all right reason; for "it is only where something must be believed, that fanaticism can raise its head." He poured the biting acid of his scorn upon the frantic running hither and thither of the professional representatives of Christianity, upon their eager hunt for "souls." They were as mad after conversions as their commercial travellers were about the getting of fresh customers. The abomination of abominations it was, however, that the different missions should snarl among one another over the newly converted, like so many dogs over a bone.

In sublime contrast to this "religion of the market-place," he set forth the teaching of the Buddha in all its serene majesty. Here every individual was made a complete, self-contained whole, and required to make no demand upon anything external in order to arrive at satisfaction. "Only when the mind feels that it has laid hold of the highest religion, only then does it desire no more, not even that all around it should recognise its religion also." He cleverly let some beams of his mental searchlight fall upon a world in which the Buddha-word, the

Dhamma alone, held sway. In his eyes it was a paradise. "For, what is it that makes of this world, a hell? Is it not because one thinks that he must help others, thinks himself obliged to do some kind of good to them? Another thinks himself under obligation to wrong and oppress others. Yet another thinks himself in duty bound to influence others? In their outcome these are all one and the same thing. There is only one way of avoiding that outcome: to remain within one's self. So soon as our spiritual centre of gravity is made to lie within ourselves, the world hangs in equipoise. So soon as there is peace within our breasts, the world is at peace, though wars rage east and west."

He next brought forward the tremendous advantage which pertains to Buddhism through its independence of faith and of God. Only in our knowing with all the powers of the understanding, faith being set aside, can everything be mastered. By his own exertions each one may lift himself out of this world of suffering, without the aid of any act of grace, without abject humiliation. Out of the very lack of every idea of God springs the iron morality of Buddhism; a morality that is planted upon the imperishable heights. Here is neither help nor encouragement nor comfort from any god. Here there is only the deed and its consequence. As surely as the falling stone reaches the earth, so surely does the consequence of the deed return to the doer thereof. Therefore is it said here, "Man be watchful. Struggle unremittingly every moment of thy life." Christianity with its begging prayers is a religion for children; Buddhism, on the contrary, clear, cold, but just, is the religion of grown men. It is the truth of the eternal law of nature set forth in the form of religion. The writer even ventured upon the expression, "The god-idea is nothing but a weakening of the moral idea."

He went on depicting, obviously with special pleasure, the quiet, peaceful progress made by Buddhism in the course of the centuries throughout great tracts of the continent of Asia, whilst Christianity had waded so deeply in blood, that it was obliged to hold its cross high, if only that it might not become bespattered with the crimson fluid.

"I now ask—'By what right does the Christian send his missionaries to Asia?' How it stands as respects his merits we have just seen. Judged by age, Christianity is a child compared with our religion, and especially as compared with the religions of our Indian motherland and of China. What is there to justify this unparalleled audacity on the part of Christianity? Nothing but its bulkier money-bags: absolutely nothing but this—that in the dice game of the world's history it has become the religion of the so-called active peoples, of those peoples who find their delight, not in repose, but in the accurst mania for work; who find their joy in working merely for the sake of working, in scraping up money merely for money's sake. Just because Christianity, like an ill-fitting shoe, has been drawn on by these peoples, therefore is it now triumphant.

There they sit, these dollar millionaires of America and of England, and, after having flung away their whole life in being successful, that is, in making money, in oppressing their neighbours and forgetting themselves, and their weary bones now aching for rest, conscience—or more often—tedium, makes itself felt, and, with a couple of millions, a mere rag of their superfluity, their past forsooth is to be covered over as with a plaster of gold! For gold, with these people, is the elixir of life. It makes the ugly beautiful; the old young; the vile virtuous. But it is the curse of this gold that, even where it is bestowed out of desire for rest, in order to produce repose, it, its own self, brings nothing but conflict and confusion."

Silananda read on with perfect composure. He would write a rejoinder. He would maintain that things were not so entirely bad as said about the money-bags; he would show that many missionaries were obliged to earn their daily bread by the work of their own hands; that it was not Christianity but Christian states that were smeared with blood. But, above all, he would call attention to the fact that the blessing of work, the blessing of spontaneous work, done out of pure love of one's neighbour, was that motive force which must always assure to Christianity the ascendency over Buddhism. He would also make some capital out of the inaccuracies of the writer. Where he said, "Conscience—or more often, tedium—makes itself felt," etc., there was a good opportunity to pull him up. No one would try to cover up his past with a plaster of millions merely out of tedium. At all events, he would go to Stevenson with the pamphlet and talk it all over with him and Miss Stevenson. He let the printed pages drop from his hand, and for a long time gazed out over the boundless ocean. What an agreeable thing life was after all!

Just as he was on the point of resuming his reading, his eye happened to glance along the street that gleamed under the hot noonday sun. In the distance he perceived a man coming, at sight of whom there strangely overcame him the feeling: "He is coming to you!" He looked keenly at him. The man did not walk: he ran, he sprang along the street. Even at that distance one could perceive the disorder of his garments. One could almost imagine one saw the panting breast, the parched tongue—heard the broken words. Suddenly a sound, almost like an oath, escaped the watcher's lips. He recognised the man. It was Sinha, the trader of the Pettah.

Silananda felt as though a piece of ice had been put down his back. Anything, anything in the world rather than another meeting with this man! There came over him, as it were, a madness. He flung into the inner part of the house, and ran distractedly up and down. He had not yet made his own that refinement of modern civilisation—to be at home and not to be at home at one and the same time. The running man, moreover, would have arrived long before he could have given instructions to his faithful old servant. Like one possessed, he seized his hat, and burst out of the house by the back entrance, through the garden, and out into the open country beyond, further and still further, until exhaustion brought him to a halt.

How long he had run he could not tell. One thing he was sure of—anywhere rather than back to the house. He was afraid that Sinha might still be waiting there. He knew what Indian patience was, so he turned in the direction of the railway station. Here, for the first time, his glance fell upon a clock. It was only a little after twelve. It was still too early for Kelani. But what was to be done? Kelani was the only place at which he now felt himself safe. In Colombo he might meet the trader anywhere in the street. He got into the train that was just starting.

On the way he became more composed.

"I am a coward," he said, scolding himself, and his anxiety gave way to anger and contempt. "It is outrageous how one man may annoy another," he thought. "But which, in this case, is the original and the worse disturber of the peace?" Again anguish wrung his heart. "My God! my

God! What will this come to?" The words resounded in him as in a place of hollowness. Only the echo rang back to him. No answer! No comfort!

He was utterly confused, and filled with conflicting emotions. At Kelani station the train was already starting off again. Only then did he observe that he had reached his destination. He jumped out hurriedly, his face in the opposite direction from the engine, stumbled, and would have been under the wheels had not a porter caught him and pulled him back with no gentle touch. The man, however, could not prevent our hero from falling in the sand of the station steps. With skinned knee, his light clothes soiled and torn, he stood there surrounded by a crowd of onlookers. He would have liked to thrash them all, but particularly he could have thrashed himself.

No one in his little kingdom had expected him quite so early. All felt themselves still at liberty. Silananda turned the corner of the first hut. A couple of old women sat there in the shade, clothed only in their loin-cloths, their withered breasts exposed. One of them was just saying with a laugh, "A porcupine sleeps with its eyes open! But have porcupines got eyes?" Both laughed in enjoyment. Then Silananda came round the corner. His look was not particularly reassuring.

"What sort of twaddle is this again?" he stormed at the women. "Can you not talk sensibly to one another? Why, do you think, did a good God give you tongues? That you might talk nonsense?"

Startled, the women jumped up, and now stood squeezed up so close against the wall, that it almost seemed as if they were endeavouring to pass from the human form into the configuration, void of perspective, of Egyptian frescoes. With their feet turned inwards, and their hands held behind their backs, they presented the very picture of confusion. One of them who had been a maid-servant for a long time in the house of a Colombo physician—the goat in this flock of lambs—said saucily—

"Sir, we were only talking together. We

already had our tongues before we began to believe in God. So it cannot have been God that gave them to us."

Beside himself, Silananda made to move towards her. She thought it better not to wait for him, but to run away.

He now raged at the others.

"As usual! Naked again, like the beasts of the field! You are Veddas; that's what you are. You are not Christians."

"Sir, it was so hot in our shifts," said one of them timidly. "We only took them off at noon. The shadows were only so long, sir—no longer."

She indicated a distance from the tip of her finger to her wrist.

"What's that you say? Too hot! Look at me! Is it too hot for me?"

"We don't know, sir."

"You never know anything. Have you ever yet seen me perspire?"

"No, sir," they all answered in chorus. "We have never seen you perspire."

Thoroughly annoyed, Silananda passed along towards the hut in which he was accustomed to gather the children together for their school lessons. It was all so terribly repugnant to him. Contrary to his usual custom, he sat down on a mat and began to brood, without being able to lay hold of a single clear thought. Out of the confusion, however—vivid, tormenting—there flashed ever and again the thought, "What business really have you here? What have you got to do with these people?"

As two struggling wrestlers, utterly exhausted, at last stand still, so to him there came at last the rest of exhaustion; he fell asleep. He dreamt that he was on a ship and was going to England. But the sea over which he sailed was red as blood. In the bow of the ship, quite alone, stood Pereira, with his back to him.

"My God!" said Silananda to himself. "How red!"

"Blood!" cried Pereira, who now stood near him. With that he laughed out loud, and the sea moaned ominously.

Silananda started up suddenly out of his sleep. The laughter still rang in his ears.

Really! There was laughing and a low murmur of speech. He rubbed his eyes and peered round. Ah! That was it! The children who were to get their lessons from him sat before the door of the hut, talking in subdued voices to one another, and passing the time with harmless jokes.

The door stood open. Unconsciously he lifted himself a little in order to spy better what they were doing. In the semi-darkness of the hut he could do so without being observed. He saw the eldest of the children, a scamp about twelve years old, showing the others something on his slate. Now the light fell upon the slate. He plainly perceived the caricature of a man dressed in European clothes, who, by the book under his arm, which projected, enormously large, before and behind, and the cane in his hand, was quite evidently meant for a schoolmaster. Obviously it was a caricature of himself, and every little fellow, as soon as he set eyes on it, began to guffaw.

This trifling occurrence, so common in the life of a schoolmaster, came to Silananda in his present mood as something almost tragic. He would have liked to weep. Suddenly it seemed as if there were wafted to him an air from those departed days when he had wept out all his little sorrows on his mother's breast. It seemed to him as if he actually inhaled the recollection, so vividly did it come before him. With an effort he pulled himself together and rose up. The buzz and laughter outside were suddenly hushed. He clearly distinguished the sound of a slate being hastily washed.

He stepped out. With surprise, he saw that the sun was near to setting.

"How long now have you been waiting?"

"Oh, sir, five minutes," said one.

"Perhaps for seven hours," said another.

"They have no idea of time, even. What can one make of such blockheads?" thought Silananda.

With sluggish brain he took up the lesson, but soon he was obliged to break off, for it was time for the evening meal, and regularity in meal hours was insisted on with special strictness. "Regularity in eating is one of the principal distinctions between the savage and the civilised man," Stevenson was accustomed to say.

Happily, it was easy, on this point at least, for the people to follow the regulations. There would have been appetite enough for an even more frequent regularity; and rice and curry, along with bananas, were provided in abundance; indeed, several times a week there was fowl.

Silananda saw that the preparations for the evening meal were being carried out on the part of the different families with some degree of ostentation, so he let the children go.

"Shameless vagabonds!" he murmured to himself, "they can do nothing but gormandise."

It was now about the time when he was accustomed to return to Colombo. To-day he had them give him a dishful of rice and curry. He had made up his mind to spend the night at Kelani.

In India there is but little difference between the menu of the rich and the poor.

For both alike, rice and curry is the Alpha and the Omega. Silananda had not forgotten how to eat rice worked up after the Sinhalese fashion into little balls with the fingers. Such was the custom in his father's house, and Revata held firmly to it. He had firmly resisted all the changes in this respect, which his son had proposed after his return from Calcutta.

When the meal was ended, Silananda called to one of the men—

"Dabra, bring me mats! I am going to sleep here."

The man's face took on a look of astonishment, but he set about to obey the command. Silananda meanwhile went for a stroll in the neighbourhood.

It was dark when he got back. In the hut there was no light. So, just as he was, he threw himself on the mats and tried to sleep. Unfortunately, the events of the day kept passing before him in a succession of vivid pictures. But he had become more composed. Again he saw the crouching Sinha through the Stevenson-Douglas lens.

"He has enjoyed the benefit of the money for so many years, and now, when one says to him, 'That's enough, friend Sinha, others want to have something, too,' he makes such a commotion!"

Something like indignation rose in him. As soon as he saw him, he would give him a good sermon, and point out to him the gift of love of the Christian religion. "But there are some people who cannot see beyond their bellies." He felt in his pocket with his hand. There were fifteen golden sovereigns there. In the dark he counted them through once more, putting them softly and carefully from one hand into the other.

At the touch of the gold, he seemed to get new life.

"I will go and see once more if everything is in order. We must really achieve something here. We really must!"

He stepped out into the open.

"Peace and rest, ye are the sweetest things on earth," the night seemed to whisper. But he did not hear it. He peered sharply about him. He saw the men still seated round a dip of coconut oil. He drew near them stealthily. While still some distance off, he heard their conversation.

"This fellow—I have forgotten his name—wanted to go hunting with me. Says I, 'Friend, I don't go. Here, at great Kalaveva, there are other devas than there are at your place up in Mihintale. You think such a lot of your wood-gods, and despise ours. That might bring you to grief, hunting.' But the fellow only laughed and said, 'Them with the elephant's trunk and the boar's hoofs!' 'All right, we'll go,' says I. We haven't gone very far, I'm telling you—hardly out of the village—when, what should we see before us but three great, big elephants, standing there as if they had been on the look-out for us! I jumps back, and runs for all I'm worth. The other fellow climbs up a tree, frightened out of his wits. And now—are you listening?—the whole three elephants make straight for the tree and try to pull it down. But now, what shall I say?—we are all good Christians here, of course, but as sure as death, the elephants don't go away until he has called on the name of the deva of Kalaveva. He told me himself, afterwards!"

A murmur of approbation followed.

"To be sure, you are Christians, but one would hardly notice it," now said Silananda, coming forward. Then, restraining himself, he went on in an unnaturally gentle voice, "Why don't you give up such silly talk and read your Bibles instead? Do you think you get food, clothing and shelter only to make pretences?"

"That is true, sir. You are right. For all the good food we get, we ought to read more in the Bible," replied one of them. "But, we don't know how it is, sir, but it makes us awfully sleepy. We always go to sleep over it."

"Because you lack true faith. What are you doing here, if you have no faith?" he cried, getting roused.

"Sir," replied the speaker, deferentially, "we didn't come here all of ourselves. But, as you know, the gentlemen in the black coats came and talked such a lot. We are all feeling quite comfortable here, if only we were left alone a bit more."

Meanwhile Silananda's eyes had grown accustomed to the darkness, and he saw, not far from the group, a man lying sleeping on the bare ground. In a rage, he pounced upon him and shook him violently.

"Hey, you! Don't you know that you are not to lie down and sleep like the beasts of the field!" he shouted at him.

The man jumped up, startled. It is Indian etiquette, even among the lower classes, that one should treat another with courtesy and consideration. To waken a sleeping man with violence is gross rudeness.

"Why were bedsteads made for you? Why were mats given you? Are you all quite irreclaimable?"

The man looked at him with defiance.

"Sir! Stop your abusing! We are not used to abusing one another here."

Silananda simply boiled with fury. "Ha, ha! Is that the way of it? You try to teach me manners, you good-for-nothing lazybones!" And, quite forgetting himself, he gave the man a blow in the face.

The man shrunk up, turned round in silence and went away. Equally silent, the others rose and followed him.

Silananda was left standing alone. Clenching his fist and grinding his teeth, he looked after them. Then he hurried to his hut, threw himself with a groan upon the mat, and lay in a semi-conscious condition until sleep brought him relief.

Next morning he woke late. With his waking, awoke also the memory of the conclusion of the previous day. His inward trouble expressed itself in a sigh. One thing stood quite clearly before him in the morning light, and that was that he was not the suitable person for this position. He must see that some one was got, even if at his own expense. He must see if he could not help in the work in some other direction. In that way everything might still be all right.

He stepped out into the open air to take a bath in the brook. He glanced round him in astonishment. Everything was so still!

"They must be occupied elsewhere," he thought. He had never before been here at this hour of the day.

When he came back from his bath, he found everything as still as before. An idea sent a sudden shiver through him. He went through all the huts, one after the other. They were all empty, but in each of them was left the complete furnishing which had been supplied them by him. The colony had been abandoned during the night. Independence was dearer to them than food and clothing. In the fewness of their needs these people are veritable kings; even when they are going about begging from door to door.

Silananda stood reflecting. All his heat and anger had flown. This serious blow had effectually cooled him.

"Up till now I have worked very well in the service of the Mission. My results are stupefying."

He pondered what was best to be done. To go at once to Colombo to Mr. Stevenson? No! He would wait here for another day.

Perhaps they would bethink themselves and come back, at least, some of them; perhaps when meal-time came, he speculated.

Dabra, the senior member of the little colony, whose office it was to serve out the daily rations, had gone too, and had taken with him, whether intentionally or unintentionally, the key of the store-house. So Silananda had to go into the village and ask for something to eat. To make sure of not receiving a refusal, he tendered the woman a piece of money.

When he had swallowed his rice, he essayed to get some information. The woman knew nothing.

"They must have gone home again," she said unconcernedly.

This day seemed to him the longest he had ever lived through. He went into one of the huts and picked up a New Testament.

"If they had even taken their Bibles with them," he thought.

He began to read, but without attention. He knew all this by heart, and the reading seemed to him like the repetition of a well-conned school lesson. He laid the book peevishly aside and went out for a walk. The villagers gaped at him. He turned aside into a by-path. Suddenly he found himself in front of the famous old Buddhist Temple of Kelani. He knew that a cousin of his father's lived here in contemplative quietude. His father had told him about him. It was a rather remarkable affair. This man, Sabakami by name, had lived a wild life in his youth, and had caused his parents nothing but care and trouble. "Since trousers and whisky have come to Ceylon, the children are not the same as they used to be towards their elders," Revata was accustomed to say.

Then, to the utter astonishment of his parents, this young man came to them one day and said, "I am tired of it now. Let me go into the monastery." His parents thought that he would just come out again next day, but no! Day after day, week after week, month after month; yes, year after year, passed away, and he remained. He had tasted of the Great Peace that comes with the renunciation of everything, even of one's own *I*—the most delicious dish which this world can offer.

Silananda looked into the broad courtyard. It looked so still and solemn. A temple servant was sweeping up the withered leaves with a broom. A yellow-clothed monk with shaven head went to and fro noiselessly from one building to another. Over everything there reigned an air of something singularly noble.

"What am I standing here for, gaping like a peasant at the annual fair?" said Silananda, angrily, to himself. He turned away and went back to his solitude.

Meanwhile noonday had come. As he passed the store-house, suddenly he noticed with surprise that the key was sticking in the lock. Dabra must have brought it back secretly during his absence. "They will have carried off everything of value," he thought. Only a few days before, he had sent a large supply of provisions from Colombo. He had hoped to find the room empty, but on opening it he saw that it was quite full and that scarcely anything was missing. Astonishing people! But Dabra, and perhaps the others also, must be still in the neighbourhood. He made up his mind to spend another night here.

The nearer it drew towards evening, the more despondent did he become. The painful idleness of this day had affected his nervous system even more than the excitement and shock of the day before. Besides this, he was one of those people over whose feelings the evening exercises a distinct influence. Added to this there was the unaccustomed loneliness. Hunger made itself felt. He went to the store-room and got himself a bunch of ripe bananas. With these he satisfied the cravings of his stomach.

After he had eaten he again took up the Bible. The first passage that met his eye was this one from the letter to the Corinthians, "But God is faithful, who will not suffer you to be tempted above that ye are able; but will with the temptation also make a way to escape, that ye may be able to bear it."

"That, to be sure, sounds very beautiful," he thought. "But what does it mean? How much, then, can a man endure? Does God know just how much we can endure?"

He started. "What are you doing here, if you have not got true faith?" he had shouted at these poor people, to whom it was an attraction to receive food and clothing. And he, the satisfied, what was he doing here, then, if he had no faith? He again thought of those days when he had wept out all his woes in his mother's lap. But now he breathed in naught of the atmosphere of that picture; he only remembered the fact. His mother truly was dead, but now he ought to lay his head on the bosom of the all-gracious God, as trustfully as a child which, in the midst of mortal danger, sleeps on its mother's breast. Did he at all possess this faith, so indispensable to the true Christian? He could have laughed that it was only now, when all was crumbling around him, that he thought of putting this question to himself. This was the very question with which he ought to have *begun* his transition to Christianity. He thought of his first conversation with Miss Stevenson. It was not learning, not zeal in work, not delight in sacrifice ; nothing made the true Christian but faith alone—this unseizable, inexplicable, unteachable, unlearnable thing. Why, then, had he left his father's religion at all, if he had not this "cork" in him which would lift him by force out of Buddhism ? Did not his mind also long for clearness, for understanding ? Was not this question, "Does, then, God know how much I can endure ?" already the hidden transition back to that system of cause and consequence which the Buddha teaches ?

Over there in Kelani the evening bells were ringing. They were rung in swift, unsolemn fashion, but the gentleness of evening fell upon and softened them also. He again thought of his father's cousin, who at that moment was perhaps sitting motionless at the door of his cell, listening to the whisper of the leaves of the Bo-tree overhead, and bathing his spirit in a meditation over the transiency of all things here below.

"He sits there and lets the world pass him quietly by. And you? Do you think you are able to turn the world in another direction? By yourself? No. But in union with others like-minded, strivers like yourself, perhaps yes. And when our united efforts have at last succeeded in putting the world into the right track, will not others come—some Hamlet natures, perhaps—and say, 'The world is out of joint. Our life's work it is to put it right'? Perhaps the Buddha was not so very far wrong in ever and again exhorting us to look after our own *I*. It might not perhaps be the most imposing task, but it is certainly the safest." That frequently-repeated phrase in the Suttas, "Here trees invite: there lonely solitudes! Devote yourselves to meditation, brothers, that sloth may not overcome you!" again came into his mind. "He makes not-doing into a deed," thought Silananda. Only now did he perceive this, and that "passivity," that "egoism," appeared to him in another light from what they did formerly. "Who knows," he thought, "whether this one deed is not greater and nobler than all those others added together? Certainly, if I do nothing but case myself up in my own web of thought, I can neither wrong another nor yet be of use to him. And myself? So long as I have been able to think, my life has been nothing but a constant effort to be useful to others. But to whom have I so far really been of any use? To a single one? And in what way? But do we really know at all what is of use to ourselves? How, then, can we know what is of use to others? I know quite well that one may come to me and say, 'How is it, friend? A man is hungry, and out of compassion I give him something to eat. Is not that a clear case of the purely useful, an unmixed benefit?' I doubt it. Perhaps it is not always best for us to be fed when we are hungry. Every sheet of paper has two sides. The upper side is not thinkable without the under side. 'I doubt'—I say, 'I doubt.'"

Thus did his thoughts torment him. Night had come, and, sleepless, he tossed about, hither and thither. His stomach also again began to make its existence felt. The bananas had alleviated his hunger, but not removed it. So he got up and fetched himself yet another bunch.

He had never liked bananas, and this large green variety was especially distasteful to him; they did not agree with him. But it could not be helped. In the village every one was asleep. So of necessity he once more eat some.

Even as he was eating the thought came to him, "How can I meet Stevenson and his daughter?" This thought now clung to him with leech-like persistence. It was like a melody with infinite variations. Almost in despair, he cried out in the words of the prophet, "Lord, deliver my soul!" But He upon whom he called came not. He did not know that this God only comes to those in whose breasts He already dwells. To crown his misery, the bananas he had eaten now also began to cause him distress. He writhed in pain, and only towards morning did he fall into a brief slumber.

Awaking late, he felt himself completely

prostrated, bodily as well as mentally. He was resolved to go back to Colombo immediately, to explain matters, resign his connection with the work, and the money once promised to the Mission he would—hm! Why give up the large sum which did not belong to him alone, to a work with which he no longer wished to have anything to do? But on what grounds could he defend his change of mind to Stevenson? Were the efforts of the Mission to be totally abandoned, simply because a young man from lack of experience in the ways of the world had made a false move? Stevenson would give a superior smile, and tell him that he was right to do just as he pleased with his own money. So he strove with himself, and the balances continually swayed first to this side and then to that.

After he had taken his bath, he again went into the village; for he could not go back to Colombo, without first getting something proper to eat. His constitution was not of those capable of enduring prolonged strain.

When he came back in order to see if everything was properly locked up, and had assured himself on the point—he had read in the papers that a number of burglaries had recently taken place in the neighbourhood—it was nearly ten o'clock. His train did not go until eleven o'clock. He had still half an hour to spare. So he sat down in front of one of the huts and began to think. "Scipio seated on the ruins of Carthage!" he said with a sigh. During the last four-and-twenty hours his thoughts had turned about in all directions like a weather-vane. Nothing else seemed left to do almost but to jest with himself.

Suddenly he heard the rattle of wheels and the brief "Hi! Hi!" of the ox-driver.

He listened. The sound came nearer. Along the road there came into sight one of those little carts drawn by a single hump-backed ox which are found in Colombo in the place of cabs. He recognised a female form in European attire. "Somebody coming to see the Kelani temple out of curiosity," he thought. Then it occurred to him that this was not the road to the temple. He got up and gazed intently at the on-coming cart. Now he recognised the face—Miss Stevenson! His heart beat like a hammer. If he had been obliged to speak at this moment, he would have choked over a simple "Yes" or "No." "God of compassion! Is this of Thy sending? Art Thou coming at my cry?" He would have liked to shout; he could have fallen on his knees and prayed. He was composed only on the merest outside when the cart came to a stop and Miss Stevenson got down. He would have gone to her assistance, but he stood still as if rooted to the spot. Only when she called out to him, "How are you, Mr. Silananda? You seemed to have disappeared from the face of the earth!" did he recover himself, move towards her, and press her hand so warmly that she looked at him in some astonishment.

"How poorly you look to-day! Have you been ill?"

"Oh, it is nothing. It will pass. Only a touch of cold."

"At last I have come to visit you here in your kingdom. We were wondering why you did not come. Mr. Douglas called early this morning asking for you. He would have sent the money to you, but his messengers were informed that you had been from home for two days. Father thought that you could only be in Kelani, so I seized the opportunity and came out in this cart. Father thought it would be much more interesting than in the train."

"Oh, certainly it is; only it is much longer on the way."

"In India, time isn't so precious as all that," she said with a laugh.

"But I shall be quite delighted to be introduced by you to your domain." She glanced round her. "How quiet everything is here!"

The words did not affect him so terribly as he had pictured beforehand. He replied with sad composure—

"I very much regret to have to tell you that the whole of the new converts left the colony secretly the night before last. The reason: my foolish behaviour. I am to blame for everything."

"Good gracious! But that hardly sounds credible!"

"The most incredible things often come about in the most disconcertingly natural fashion. A single box on the ear set this machinery in motion and brought it to its present issue. It has become clear to me that this is not the field of work adapted to me. I have made up my mind to give place to some one else."

"But, Mr. Silananda, you are surely going too far! Everything can surely be put right again. The worst is not that people should make mistakes, but that one should never learn anything from one's mistakes."

"Certainly that is the worst of all, and I am firmly resolved not to commit that worst of all mistakes!"

She saw that his thoughts were moving steadfastly in their own groove. Obviously it would not be easy to turn him aside. But she must try everything. Apart from the money—certainly, she ought to think of the money: it was not for her, but for the good cause—apart from the money, her father had told her that Silananda was the only scientifically-educated Sinhalese they had at the time working for the Mission. The others were, if not in a material way, at least in mind, rather mediocre.

"But what have you been doing here alone all day and all night?"

"I have been waiting to see if the people would perhaps come back."

"What thoughts you must have had!"

He was like the thirsty plant that receives a drop of dew from heaven. The most potent balm for a wounded heart is a word of understanding. Had she said, "How unspeakably sorry I am for you!" or "How you must have suffered!" it would have been nothing more than the correctly made out form of a courteous reply. But when she simply said, "What thoughts you must have had!" it seemed as it were to cover all that had been endured in those hours of distress. He seized her hand with a sudden motion. The tears welled into his eyes.

She stood a moment in perplexity; then she cried briskly—

"But now, before anything else, back to Colombo. There everything can be made all right again. There is room in my cart for four. We will go back together."

These little carts have two long seats for two persons. He took his place opposite to her. With a "Hi! hi!" the journey began, and the little hump-backed ox trotted merrily off.

Silananda's sudden transport appeared to be followed by as deep a depression. He sat like one overwhelmed, and kept his eyes steadily on the floor of the vehicle. It would have been impossible, at least according to the views of a European lady, to travel in a situation like this all the way from Kelani to Colombo. It is one of the misfortunes of our world that, in the presence of a lady, silence always says something! How much less misfortune might have happened to the world, if only ladies and gentlemen could sit beside one another without speaking.

So, after they had travelled about a quarter

of the distance without Silananda's having given any sign of starting a conversation, Miss Stevenson began—

"Really, Mr. Silananda, I can't bear to see you sitting like that. Do say something!"

He looked up astonished. He had never before had closer relations with European ladies, and this way of addressing him was so un-Indian, so provoking. What could he say just then when he was depressed? The demand struck him rather unpleasantly. Does one then require of a sick bird that it should sing?

"Please tell me something of your own life," she persisted. "It interests me so much."

Again he looked at her. "What shall I tell you about my life? There is nothing to tell. What there is you already know. But," he continued, and his form resumed its elasticity, "I would ask you to tell me something of your life. For the moment, there is nothing else in the world with which you could rouse my interest."

She glanced somewhat hastily at the sun and at her sun-shade, although she sat completely in the shade. For a moment it seemed as if she would evade his request; then she said earnestly—

"I will tell you because you have suffered. Not as if I had anything great to tell, but, all the same, I say, I only tell you, because you have suffered. You must know," she continued quite calmly, "a girl of the ordinary stamp has a life story only when there is love in it."

He sat motionless, his eyes fixed upon her.

"About five years ago,"—she broke off. "I am not beginning with my life but with my history."

He nodded.

"Well, about five years ago, I went from Ceylon to England—it was in March, and a voyage over the Indian Ocean at that time of the year is a pleasure trip—and we had many birds of passage on board. I went on a German ship because they are the largest. There I made the acquaintance of a German gentleman, with whom I apparently would never have exchanged a word during the whole voyage if he had not happened to be my neighbour at table. I do not know any German—generally speaking my compatriots are by far the laziest in the learning of languages—and he spoke English very badly, but, strangely enough, in one evening we were intimate friends.

"You must not think that I had had little to do with gentlemen before this. Quite the contrary; but, in spite of long acquaintance, they had never come half so close to me as this man, with his scarcely comprehensible English, had done in a couple of hours. Both of us of a reflective and religious turn of mind, we soon found a great number of points where we had mutual contact. We could go a long way with one another in our discussions, but on one point our ways always parted. He had a completely established, perfectly deliberate tendency to concentrate all his thought, all his mental activity, inwards, upon his own *I*. I had an unshakable belief in the blessedness, the necessity of work; in activity expended in an outward direction; in the love of humanity.

"No part of my life can be compared in sweetness with the period of these relations. Together we watched the rising and the setting of the sun, and that seemed to knit us still closer together. If we were kept apart from one another during the day by others, in the evening each of us sought the other as the lamb seeks its mother. Each of us knew that we loved the other, without a single word of it having fallen from either's lips."

Suddenly breaking off her story, she said lightly—

"It has always seemed to me grossly unnatural in the writers of love-stories, when they leave their lovers in doubt as to their mutual feelings. It is with true love as with that new chemical substance which one sees shining even with one's eyes shut."

She laughed gaily; constrained, he joined in.

"You see," she went on, "this side remark has saved me from the melancholy which else must surely have fallen upon me at the conclusion of my story. So I will now go on with it. In Genoa most of the passengers got off. We remained with the ship. To cut it short, at Gibraltar we plighted our troth. At Southampton we bought rings, and on the same day he continued his journey to Germany, whither urgent business called him.

"Our marriage was to take place soon, and in Ceylon, in fact. There was not a single obstacle. I, indeed, was without means, but he was rich. Immediately upon his arrival in Hamburg, I received from him a letter, which will be my most cherished possession as long as I live. I felt how high he stood above me in intellectual attainments, but, as a not unworthy set-off, I felt able to give myself entirely to him to command. There followed some shorter letters, evidently written in haste.

"Meanwhile, almost three months had passed and with inexplicable timidity I had so far said nothing about it to my father. Then there came one day a longer letter, in which my betrothed laid before me in marvellous fashion, how that now, since I was absent, his tendency towards reflection had again got the upper hand, and how even his most precious possession, his love for me"—she uttered the words in a dry, almost business-like tone—"had not escaped the destructive influence. He felt himself unable to exchange the comfort of single life for the cares of married, of family life. He was ashamed from his heart of the presumptuous word, and to me alone would he venture to utter it—he felt himself above love. That's all. I have never heard another word from him, notwithstanding—— You see just a jilted person before you. It wasn't so interesting as you had expected. The only interesting thing for both of us is this, that my love for humanity has not suffered in the least; indeed, it has perhaps become more intense."

Silananda's only answer was to take her hand.

"Miss Stevenson"—his voice was completely changed in his emotion—"these two days it has seemed to me as if I were forsaken both by God and man. I prayed, but without result. Then you came, and I knew that it was God who sent you; that my prayer was answered. Miss Stevenson, do not reject me, you cannot reject me; for God Himself has sent you to me. Will you be my wife?"

She had turned deathly pale.

"In God's name, Mr. Silananda, what are you saying? Why do you do this to us both? Do you not see that, even if my liking for you were of that kind, I dare not give you an answer to-day? Your present declaration is only the reaction of the last two days."

"Oh, Miss Stevenson, do not think that! Not that! I have loved you from the first moment that I saw you. But, God help me! I would have moved near you until grey old age, without even venturing to ask for your hand, if it had not been impressed upon my very soul—'God sends her to thee! Take her! She is thine.'"

"My poor, poor friend," she said, "it is a

dangerous thing to listen for God's voice so long as all that is human in the heart is not silent."

"Oh, is that so?" he said with bitterness. "My heart then has been a deceived deceiver."

"And then," she went on softly, "true love never dies. The barren soil of memory suffices it for deeper devotion."

He scarcely seemed to hear her. He sat there all sunk together.

"Woe is me!" thought Henrietta. "If we had only travelled from Kelani to Colombo in silence! My talking has spoiled everything."

She subsided, when suddenly he again began—

"Miss Stevenson, I ponder and ponder, and cannot come to any conclusion."

She looked at him rather anxiously. She did not know what he wished to say.

"You see," he went on, "I cannot help myself; the events of the past few days seem to me to be a punishment for something that has happened in the past. My whole life at the present moment lies before me like an open book, from the time when I first began to be conscious of living, and it is only that time that can enter into the question. My life has always been so childishly simple, that I think I can myself reckon up the rewards and punishments in it."

"Mr. Silananda, do not sin against your soul! That no man can do! That belongs to God alone!"

"You say, 'That belongs to God alone,' which means, otherwise expressed, 'It is wholly incomprehensible to us.' In that case we dare hardly speak at all of reward and punishment, for these are things which every one thinks himself able to understand, thinks himself obliged to understand. It is much more natural to consider that we are dealing with nothing else but the manifested effects of concealed causes."

She would have interrupted him, but he was evidently exerting himself to hold fast to a definite thought.

"One moment, Miss Stevenson! In my

life there is only one thing about which I am not clear as to whether it deserves reward or punishment, from which consequently I might possibly deduce all the misery of these last days; and that is, my going over to Christianity. Now, consider it in the most indulgent manner," he went on in the tone of one giving a demonstration, "it is still wholly impossible that the Christian God should punish any one because he forsakes his own religion and goes over to Him."

"Father in heaven, how you speak!"

"How else can a man speak if he would arrive at clearness of mind? How can he arrive at clearness of mind if he remains buried over the ears in the things about which he desires clearness? So, I lay Christianity aside for a while in order to be able to consider it with impartiality."

"You have never truly possessed it. Christianity cannot be put off and on like a coat. And were you to try a hundred times over to place yourself in an impartial position towards it, if there is faith within you, then Christianity is within you also."

"That means, in other words, Faith hinders me from considering clearly and logically that which I believe. A dangerous property!"

"That precisely is called faith which cannot be unravelled by reasoning; only as long as it remains unravelled is it faith. This is just the seal and sign of the believer, that of his own free will he renounces this unravelling."

"This is too much, too much. You mean by that, that if I had proper faith, I would think, with everything which comes to me obviously undeserved, 'To be sure I am not aware of having committed any offence, but it is enough that God knows why He is punishing me!' But is not that unworthy of a man? Would not even an intelligent dog get indignant at such treatment?"

"Stop!" she cried sternly. "It is terrible to listen to one void of faith, reasoning about faith."

"Perhaps," he replied almost in a friendly tone, "it is still more terrible when the person of faith reasons about the lack of faith. For the believer always has the passion to encompass the other, whilst the unbeliever, at least the meditative variety of unbeliever, always has a tendency to withdraw into himself; obviously the less dangerous of the two tendencies."

"You did not know that only a few weeks ago," she said somewhat sarcastically.

"No," he replied quietly. "One often learns in one night more than in a century. Look here! If I were to represent the believer as a sculptor might, I would represent him as a human figure, which, with eyes fixed upon the far distance, mouth open as if to speak, arms spread wide, and fingers apart, flees with huge strides over hill and dale, over sea and land, over whole worlds. The unbeliever, however, I would picture as a human figure, sitting motionless with legs crossed, arms held close to the body, fingers firmly entwined in one another, mouth closed, and eyes lowered. Such a one thinks inwardly, speaks inwardly, works inwardly."

"Just say, 'The Buddha.'"

He smiled. "But I am always straying away from my line of thought. Once more: in the whole of my life there has been nothing doubtful but my conversion. Since that event I have been out of harmony with my home circle; since then I have often had quarrels with my father, I have caused him pain; taken altogether, a whole host of things deserving of punishment. But they have all been the inevitable results of my conversion. How can God consider me at fault for having turned to Him? But above all, how *can* He punish me for these faults? For I am suffering pain for every past fault. That is unjust. Injustice, however, is not consistent with the character of God. That, however, another god is very angry with this God on account of my conversion, and punishes me for it—this also is not possible; for God is precisely the unique, the One and only, without shadow of duality. If there should exist besides this one God, yet another god, then both, of necessity, must be false gods—that is to say from our point of view—delusions and frauds."

"The pure heathen, or else madness," thought Henrietta.

"Much more plausible it is," he continued thoughtfully, "to look at the whole of this business from a purely mathematical or scientific standpoint, and to say to one's self, 'What I have met with in these last days must be the effect of some kind of cause.' The only cause I can imagine is my conversion to Christianity. Moreover, this conversion, in turn, is nothing but the result of some still earlier cause. This cause is my restless nature, ever craving some new thing, never satisfied with what it has got. This again must be the effect of some previous cause. But here, I already overleap the boundaries of this present life and with my understanding seize the fact of an earlier life, and so on, *ad infinitum*, beyond your creation of the world, still further and further, backwards and backwards. 'Without beginning and without end is this Samsara.'"*

"You are giving there a very sorrowful presentation of Kamma," she said coldly.

* The round of birth and death.

"That is evident," he went on, speaking more to himself than to her. "What matters it that thus I must give up this hypothesis of a beginning in a creation of the world, of an end in a heavenly life? What does it matter, if only my sense of what is just is satisfied? Rather will I be squashed flat under the wheel of necessity than tremble for ever beneath the lash of a God. The life of a dog!"

"Mr. Silananda," Miss Stevenson now began, "you have just said that your conversion has led you to all your faults; that your faults of these latter days were the inevitable result of your conversion. I ask you, 'Why inevitable?' Why are you not honest with yourself? Why do you not say to yourself that all your errors were only the results of your half-heartedness, the consequences of your lack of inward purity? You talk as if you had in you the holy backbone of faith; in reality, however, there has only been the confusion of unbelief. Why should you be surprised that every activity of your so-called faith, every movement of this feeble backbone of yours should cause you grief and pain? Because you are only now beginning to put to yourself a question which you ought to have asked yourself at the very outset—that is why you have suffered. And, after all, what have you really suffered in these last days? Is not this grief only the reflex of your half-heartedness? You have given money to a merchant and now do not know which is better: to leave it in the shop or to devote it to the service of God. You have been overhasty, and have trifled with people's sympathies. Why? Just because you came here in a troubled state of mind and full of doubts. You have passed two bad nights, have fared somewhat poorly; what further cause need be looked for? Just wait until the real great sorrow of your life comes upon you, and the answer which your innermost then supplies—give heed to it!"

He looked at her in astonishment, almost in admiration. How was it possible that everything in the world became otherwise with every fresh light thrown upon it? What then had really come over him? Nothing. And this "nothing" again was only the result of his own inner half-heartedness. This must all be put to rights again. Yes, fortunately he could say that his inward self, by such a trivial occasion, had received this stimulus to reflection upon itself. Whosoever only once begins to ask: "How stands it with me?" has already done the larger part of the work. Whoso only begins to seek for himself, seeking, he finds himself. Here, to seek is only a latent form of finding one's self.

To him there was something peculiarly sweet and restful in the thought. He experienced an indefinable gratitude, he knew not towards whom. He quite forgot his companion's presence and followed up his thought. He was like a man who has escaped from the fury of wind and storm, and now in a sheltered valley way hears the roaring of the tree-tops high over his head.

Suddenly Henrietta again began. "Mr. Silananda, I was unjust to you just now; forgive me!"

He made no answer. He smiled a smile so still, so peculiar, that she knew not whether he smiled to her or to something else away in the distance behind her.

Quite abruptly he then began. "Did you not say just now, Miss Stevenson, that the money is ready, in Mr. Douglas's hands?"

"Quite correct!"

He tore a leaf out of his note-book, wrote something on it, and handed it to her.

She read, "This is to notify Mr. Douglas to hand over the three thousand rupees to the bearer."

"Mr. Silananda," she said, giving him back the paper, "I cannot now accept your magnanimous gift. I must ask you to send it to my father or to Mr. Ross."

His face took on such a disconsolate expression, that her sympathy quite overpowered her.

"Give it," she said. "I will hand it to my father myself."

"How good you are, how sympathetic!" he said, without a trace of bitterness.

Such warmth shone in his beautiful clear

eyes, that she felt it penetrating her, even to her heart. She lowered her eyes. Her breath came fast.

"Mr. Silananda," she said, still with lowered glance, "how infinitely sad you have made me to-day!"

He did not in the slightest degree possess the capacity for coining the moments as one might coin gold pieces. Perhaps, also, his mind was now soaring too high in the ether to be able to bestow any attention on the finesse of this low earth. He answered simply——

"And you have been so infinitely kind to me."

"Was I really kind?"

She looked at him smiling. "Oh, you have been as kind to me as a mother." He now knew to whom his feeling of thankfulness was directed. "I admire you beyond my power to say. You stand so high above me."

Her smile disappeared. "You are a seeker. Do you think that that is so little?" She glanced sideways into the road as she spoke. "We are now quite near to Colombo. How fast the little creature has run!"

"May I accompany you now to your father's?"

"You will find him at home at this very moment."

As they entered, they found Mr. Stevenson and Mr. Ross in the sitting-room.

"Just see!" said Mr. Ross, when general greetings were over, "you have settled down in Kelani so long that Miss Stevenson herself has had to go and fetch you away! I hope you have had a pleasant return journey?"

"Yes, thank you!" replied Silananda, in some confusion. His nature made it impossible for him to pay back this man in his own coin.

"Yes, yes!" He fixed his eyes on him. "Well, how are things in general getting on? You were so very kind as to leave us for three whole days entirely without news."

"The colony in Kelani is no longer in existence. All the new converts have left it secretly."

"What's that you say?"

"Unfortunately, I have to inform you that in anger I gave one of the people a box on the ear. That was the cause of it."

A pause ensued.

"A fatal thing, most certainly!" at last said Stevenson.

"Young man," Ross now began unctuously, "if you regretted your promise to us with regard to the money, all you had to do was simply to let us know, and the affair was ended. Why snatch at means like these?"

Silananda looked at him speechlessly.

The blood shot to Henrietta's face, and, turning quickly to Ross, she gave him the sheet of paper. She had come with the firm intention to give it to her father only on the morrow, in order to give time for a change of mind on Silananda's part, but in her emotion she now forgot her resolve.

Mr. Ross read. Somewhat disconcerted he said—

"Then I have been quite mistaken. But you must not take it too much to heart. Does Mr. Douglas know your signature?"

"Yes, he has it beside him."

"Then I will just go over to him immediately."

He took his leave rather hastily.

"Dear me, Mr. Silananda, tell me all about it!" cried Mr. Stevenson, when Mr. Ross had gone.

"Your daughter knows everything. She will tell you about it better than I am able to do just at the moment. I am going home."

"Mr. Ross has wounded you. His intentions are good, but he lacks delicacy. I hope I shall see you here again very soon."

When Silananda entered the house, his servant looked at him in astonishment.

"Has my father come back yet?"

"No, sir!"

He briefly ordered his midday meal and threw himself into a chair on the veranda. It was the very same chair which he had risen out of in such haste two days ago.

Mr. Ross's final reproach seemed to him so frightful, that he only wondered; he could not get indignant. "If even the deed that springs from the noblest emotion is not safe from being dragged in the mud, what is the use of busying one's self on behalf of any object?" he thought.

After he had eaten he went to his bedroom. On the table there he found a letter with a Sinhalese superscription awaiting him. It was from the merchant Sinha. Silananda read—

"Sila, have mercy! On my knees I implore you by all that is holy and dear to you, I implore you, have mercy! Have mercy on the poor wife and on the four little things! No religion, not even thine, can teach that evil deeds bring forth good fruit. Why wilt thou do thyself hurt? Sila, if ever you wish to sleep quietly again, come! Come to-day, no matter how late it may be! Save me from these tigers who strangle men in the name of the law!"

Utterly taken aback he let the letter fall. So all these Englishmen had deceived him. But Miss Stevenson! She could not have deceived him! She knew no better; but he—Oh, he! He was the guilty one: on his head the sword would whistling fall!

Like a raging animal he burst out of the house. As he went out, he asked the servant—

"How long has the letter been lying there?"

"Since the day before yesterday, sir."

Once out on the street, he began to reflect over what was to be done. To get the money back again, or go and see the merchant first?—To Sinha before everything.

Arrived at the outskirts of Colombo, he took a rickshaw. It was late in the afternoon, and the Pettah was thronged like an ant-hill. Approaching the bazaar, the rickshaw coolie could scarcely make any progress. Now he was at the corner. Breathless with suspense, he kept his eyes fixed in the direction where Sinha's stall must soon come into sight. But now—merciful heaven! the shop was shut. He looked once again. There was no doubt about it; it was Sinha's shop. He stopped the rickshaw and went over to one of the neighbouring stalls. In as careless a tone as he could muster, he asked:

"What's the matter with Sinha?"

"Oh, a man from the court came yesterday. I don't know what you would call him. A Bombay man bought up everything. Sinha cried a good deal."

"Did the Bombay man take away everything?"

"How could he, sir? It is all inside yet."

Not a moment was to be lost. Off to Mr. Douglas at once. Business hours were over, but Mr. Douglas was so uncommonly kind as to permit Silananda to speak to him. The money had already been taken away by Mr. Ross at midday.

Then to Mr. Stevenson's house. He saw nobody as he went along, although his eyes were directed into the midst of the throng. He laughed grimly to himself. "What then had happened? Oh, nothing had happened. That a whole family had just about been ruined was outside the question!"

At Stevenson's house there was again a gathering of the missionaries to consider events at Kelani. Silananda asked to see

Mr. Stevenson immediately. He came out. In broken words—Stevenson must have divined a good deal—he made it known that he must have the money back again.

"Dear Mr. Silananda, this is a bad affair," said Stevenson, thoughtfully. "But come with me. I will bring it before the meeting at once."

In a few words he informed the assembled company of Silananda's trouble. A general silence fell upon the meeting. Mr. Ross began—

"Suppose it should really be the case that a third party is hurt, that would certainly be very sad. But, young man," he turned to Silananda and continued in stern tones, "you really must not imagine that you can make our whole society the plaything of your humours. To-day you give, to-morrow you take back again. The money has come into our possession, and the question is this, gentlemen: 'Have we the right to give it up again?' Nothing here can be worse than a policy of blind sentiment. If this Sinha has really become bankrupt, who can say that it is just this three thousand rupees that have broken his neck? Who can say that this sum, if we give it back, will not simply disappear among his other assets, and thus do the man no good at all? Our plans, on the other hand, which serve the noblest ends, the ends of the highest philanthropy, would be frustrated for years to come, perhaps for ever, by this step. Taking into consideration all the factors in the case, there cannot be the slightest doubt which side the scales incline to, in this affair. Gentlemen, we must not be forgetful of our duty, we must not trample our ideals under foot, merely to save a trader in the Pettah from problematical ruin."

"But the Kelani scheme is now quite at an end," said one.

"All the more do we need the money in order better to establish it again. And why is it at an end? Picture to yourself, gentlemen," he continued keenly, "some one blunders with his foot right into a little pool of water. What is the result? All the water splashes out, the puddle is empty. But little by little it all gathers together again of itself. It will be the same here, be sure of that! Perhaps even to-morrow we shall have some to look after again. I know," he proceeded in a louder voice, "what my duty, what the duty of all of us is—to do good to others and to help them to the best of our ability. 'Love of Humanity' stands emblazoned on our banner. I, for one, am firmly resolved to fulfil this duty to the uttermost. But do you call it fulfilling our duty, if of our own free will, we allow ourselves to be deprived of the means of fulfilling it?"

He looked round him to read the faces of his colleagues.

"Mr. Silananda, I know that you on your part have almost forced the money upon us. Would it be quite impossible for you now to get the money from some other quarter? Is it absolutely necessary that you should take back the money from us?"

This last reason seemed to give the finishing stroke. Surely it was easier for him than for the Mission to get another three thousand rupees. Ross saw how things were going.

"I now ask the gentlemen to state their opinion."

All five were in favour of retaining the money.

As dumbly as he had entered, Silananda left the room, Stevenson accompanying him. He had not been quite prepared to oppose anything to this latter line of reasoning. Even from Mr. Ross' mouth it had seemed to him quite justified.

Once outside, Mr. Stevenson said in a subdued voice—

"Dear Silananda, believe me, nothing can be done. We could not do otherwise. You are in a bad position, I know"—there was a ring of confidence in his voice—"but what could I do? Mr. Ross would say the most harsh things about me, not only here, but also in England. Who knows what motives would be imputed to me? Reasons are picked up anywhere and everywhere for the most incredible combinations." He brushed a speck of dust from the sleeve of his black coat. "One must be very prudent, both as an official and as the father of a family." He continued to brush at his coat-sleeve, although there was no longer a speck of dust there. "Moreover, you yourself must admit that his reasons were quite just. What a pity that my daughter is not here!"

Back to the house, then. One thing only was now clear to him: his father must give. After all, it was not for the Mission, but for Sinha. His father, however, was not at home. How utterly fatal! And any possibility of getting the money in his name, without his signature, was unknown to Silananda.

He turned home again, since he did not know where else to go. With delight he learned that his father had just returned.

"Father is ill," said Amba.

"How? Father is never ill."

"We were obliged to stand for hours in the broiling sun in the court-yard of the monastery, which is surrounded by buildings, you know. It was like an oven, and we were all crowded together, and had eaten nothing in the morning."

"But why not?" he asked in astonishment.

"Because it is so meritorious." She was surprised that he remained quite calm. "Then, all of a sudden, there came a downpour of rain. Father at once began to feel cold. I saw that he was shivering, and said, 'Let us go, father.' But as he did not answer me, and did not even look at me, I said no more."

"Where is he now?"

"In his bedroom."

"Amba, I really must see him. It is about things of the greatest importance, about Sinha."

"Oh!" she said, ready to cry, "I read the letter in your room. It lay open on the ground."

He made no answer but went to the old man's bedroom.

He found his father, contrary to his custom, quite wrapped up, seated on the edge of his bedstead. Silananda knew that lying down during the day was a horror to him.

"Father, I am very, very sorry to find you ill."

"Sadhu, my son! I am glad that you have come to me."

"Father, I would not willingly disturb you, but it can't be helped. Sinha, by my thoughtlessness, has been plunged into the greatest misfortune. Father, give me the three thousand rupees so that I may make good again what I have spoiled."

The old man did not look up. In silence, apparently unmoved, he sat there. At last, he said in a peaceful voice—

"I have considered. It won't do."

"Why not, father?" Anxiety and excitement gave his son's voice a touch of vehemence.

"It is not your place to ask that," the old man replied.

With that he got up, evidently with the intention of leaving the room and thus putting an end to the interview.

His son stepped towards him. "Father," he cried in an almost unrecognisable voice, "do you then wish to drive your son mad?"

Had Revata looked up at this moment, this face would have startled him, would have moved him. He would have yielded, and the deliverance of his son . . . ? But he kept on moving away, his eyes steadily lowered. Almost beside himself with rage and despair, Silananda seized his arm violently—

"Father, do have pity!"

As if to give force to his words, he gave the old man a jerk. Revata staggered, slipped, and fell heavily, his head striking the sharp corner of the bedstead. He picked himself up at once. A stream of blood was trickling over his face. Silananda stood like one paralysed.

"Call Amba!" said the old man.

Stricken dumb, Silananda ran out.

That night Revata was taken with severe fever accompanied by hallucinations. The Sinhalese physician was called in. Revata had always strictly forbidden the calling in of an English doctor. This man prepared a draught and let a large quantity of blood. But still the fever did not fall, the hallucinations continued, and the patient's strength sank rapidly. By the next morning the issue was beyond doubt. The whole day Revata lay muttering, and picking with his fingers. At evening he became quiet; death was coming on. He died without having exchanged word or look with his children. Dumb, tearless, both sank down beside the bed. Since the day before, they had not spoken a word except such as could not be avoided.

Silananda now got up. He looked thin and aged.

"Sister," he said quietly, "I am to blame for everything; I am the murderer. I have had no mercy on myself."

Then the girl's convulsed heart opened. Weeping aloud, she flung her arms round her brother's neck.

"Oh my good, noble brother, what has come over thee?" she sobbed. "Oh if you had never set eyes on these people!"

"Who knows, who knows!"

Even in her sorrow she noticed the peculiarity of his tone of voice. She looked up.

"Why do you not weep with me, Sila? Do weep!" she cried to him coaxingly, anxiously.

"Amba, my heart has wept the whole night and all this day—blood! Sister! It is now enough. Miss Stevenson said to me, 'When the real sorrow comes, then ask your innermost, and the answer which it gives you, give heed to it!' I have given heed to it, Sister! The god who speaks to these does not answer me. What have I to do with a dead god? There is only one fire which can burn my guilt to ashes—not the fire of prayer, not the fire of self-mortification, not the fire of love; there is only one fire that can do it—the fire of knowledge. I now have got faith in the Tathāgata. My mind is easy. I shall understand. And understanding, this miserable *I* will disappear, and with it, all my guilt."

"Brother, my very heart rejoices."

"The coming day still belongs to life. This body must be given back to earth, and the merchant Sinha must have six thousand rupees. The old Silananda gives them to him. The new Silananda busies himself over no man's affairs, since he has enough to do with his own. But the new Silananda knows that in this way he best serves, not only himself, but the world. To-morrow I enter the monastery at Kelani. And you, my sister?"

"I go with thee, brother!"

NALA THE SILENT

THIS narrative begins like a fairy tale. There was once a man who lived in the sacred city of Kandy, not very far away from the temple of the Sacred Tooth-relic. He had a stall in the Street of the Law, where he earned his daily bread by honest dealing.

One day, as this man began to feel that he was drawing near to his latter end, he said to his son, "Nala, my son, thou knowest that thy mother and thy sisters have already left us and passed on." He meant, they had died and had obtained another re-birth. "And this my wretched bodily form also, this collection of Sankhāras,* is on the eve of dissolving and coming together again to make a new form, for, as yet, Nibbāna for me is far away. Now, I have much revolved

* The impermanent components of things.

in mind as to whether I should make over all my worldly goods to the temple of the Sacred Tooth, or leave them behind to thee. As, however, I but just now asked thee concerning the matter and thou didst answer, 'As it pleases thee, father,' I saw by that, that thou possessest the blessed gift of reflectiveness, and that thou wilt not use the money merely to heap together still more. Therefore I will leave my all to thee, not that thou mayest indulge in idleness, but that the life of reflection may be made easy for thee. For it is not easy to be reflective when one must hunt for one's daily bread. But, two things you must promise me faithfully and solemnly. First, that you will always bear in mind that saying of the Buddha, 'To whom not anything is dear—to him not anything is grievous!' and, second, that you will never put a question to a woman."

The son faithfully and solemnly promised to observe these two things as a sacred vow his whole life long.

Thereupon the father went on. "This

have I required of thee, because I have left to thee all my possessions, when it would have been much more advantageous for me and have insured me a better re-birth, if I had made a gift of them to the temple. For thou knowest, my son, that in death the paths of parents and children are divided, and that nothing goes with us save our own deed. Now, however, I would give thee wise counsel which thou mayst heed or not as thou choosest. Do not carry on this business which I have followed. My Kamma it was to have wife and children; therefore was I obliged to follow a business in order to support them. Man, however, lives most innocently when he lives by the soil. Thus living, he works least harm to others."

This counsel also the son promised to follow.

Some time after, the old man died. The son mourned for him in a fitting manner, but, because he was a good son, he found comfort in thoughts of the transiency of all that has arisen. Then he took all that his father had left behind to him, and bought himself a little house and a piece of land up on the farther side of the mountain, living there all by himself, lonely but contented. When he looked down over the great plain at his feet, upon which the distant hillocks seemed as ships upon an ocean, and the streams like veins of silver, then was his mind filled with joy and peace. Day after day he thought to himself, "What a splendid life is this! To whom not anything is dear—to him not anything is grievous!"

Now it happened one day, that he saw in his garden a little bird, which was not bright and gleaming like the other birds, but coloured plain black and white, and it rocked its tail up and down in a way that was a pleasure to see.

Nala thought, "What a funny little fellow thou art, to be sure!" and stood stock still, so as not to disturb it. Then the bird began to hop quickly all around, snapping up insects, from one end of the garden to the other. Then it would stand still for a little while, its legs thrust saucily apart, and look trustfully at Nala. Or it would perch on a spray and preen itself. With its beak it would work at its feathers for as far as it could get at them, but it looked at its drollest when pecking at the feathers up round its throat. Anon it would stretch out a wing and vigorously explore beneath it, and then repeat the operation with the other. But when it lifted its little foot and began to scratch its head, first on one side and then on the other, Nala could hardly withhold himself from laughter.

When it had hunted in this fashion for a couple of hours to its entire satisfaction, it flew twittering away.

Next morning Nala is sitting quietly in his garden looking down over the plain, when suddenly the little bird is there again, and proceeds to go all through the same performance.

Thus it went every day, week after week. His first glance, when he stepped into his garden in the mornings, was for the bird; and if it was there, he kept carefully to that side of the garden where it did not hunt, or else he kept wholly to the house so as not to disturb it. When in its eagerness it came close up to him, he would say, "Just look what a brave little chap it is!" And at times when he did not venture into the garden for fear of disturbing it, he would say to himself with a smile of self-satisfaction, "Here too the saying holds good, 'Who owns the house—he keeps away!'"

Thus passed many weeks. One day, however, the bird was missing. Nala waited and waited, but all in vain. The next day and the next it was the same; the little bird came not. Then did Nala become sad; food no longer tasted good in his mouth; and the rising and the setting of the sun spoke to him no more.

"What can have happened to the little bird?" he asked himself. "Has it turned faithless to me, because it has found a better hunting-ground? Has it been devoured by a hawk or a snake? Has it been caught in a snare?" One possibility was as painful to think of as any other. Then he noticed that something was dear to him; hence now he suffered this grief.

"How truly," he thought, "did the Exalted One speak, when he said, 'To whom not anything is dear—to him not anything is grievous.' I must keep a more careful watch over myself." In secret, however, he still waited for the little black and white bird with its little bobbing tail, and gazed inquiringly at every feathered creature that came near.

Then one day he beheld how a sparrow fed its young. The young one sat upon a tender branch, while the old one fluttered anxiously over him, until it had got the dainty bite safely into the beak that gaped for it; and this was repeated again and again.

Nala sat reflecting. "How wonderful!" he thought. "It is not enough that this mother should deny herself the food and give it to her young one instead; she also thinks it no trouble to flutter over him and put it right into his beak. She does not say to her young one, 'You there! Come down from your branch! you are making my work too difficult for me!' Wonderful! truly wonderful!" And with this his heart became full of love on account of the little bird.

Nala's thoughts now roved hither and thither from morning until evening; at night he slept. Finally he said to himself: "It will be much better if I take to myself a wife. It does not seem to me to be a good thing to set one's self against nature. I can still keep my two vows. It is not forbidden to honour and esteem one's wife, and I will never put questions to her."

When he had thus made up his mind, he seated himself in front of his door by the roadside. He thought, "Perhaps the right one will pass by here." There passed, however, up and down, only a carrier, or an old woman with a basket on her head. They said nothing but "Good day!" and passed on.

When now he understood that the thing was impossible that way, he walked down into the town. He was, however, of a shy disposition and scarcely dared to look at a woman.

On the outskirts of the town he came to a hut standing all by itself. Before the door a girl sat, in front of her a little black board upon which lay a lump of sugar-cane, a bit of buffalo horn, and a piece of ivory.

Nala stopped and viewed everything. He wanted desperately to ask what it all meant but dared not.

When he had thus stood in silence for some time, the girl began—

"What are you standing there for without asking what this means?"

"I may not put questions," said Nala.

"Why not?" she laughed.

"Because I have solemnly promised it to my father."

"Oh, so you are Nala from the Street of the Law!" the girl laughed loudly.

"I don't live in the Street of the Law," said Nala. "I live up on the other side of the mountain and have a pretty little house there."

"It doesn't matter. I know now; you are Nala." And with that she laughed again, showing all her teeth.

Nala would dearly have liked to ask, "Why do you laugh like that?" but he dared not. She went on—

"People say that you may never ask a woman any kind of question. But how will you ever get a wife, if you may not ask her whether she will have you or no?"

Nala received a shock. Was that really the case? He had never thought of it that way. He rubbed his ear and, visibly perturbed, gazed at the girl.

"Come, now," she said, "perhaps things won't be so bad after all. You will surely find one if you only look in the proper place. But, if you may not ask any questions, I will explain to you the meaning of the board here. The sugar-cane means, 'Sweet must my lover be like the sugar-sap.' The buffalo-horn means, 'Strong must he be like the buffalo.' The ivory means, 'Noble and wise must he be like the elephant.'"

"Heavens!" thought Nala, "if all women are so exacting, how will even a man who may ask get a wife?" That the girl had laughed at him vexed him sorely.

He said to himself, "Nala, you will never, never get a wife in Kandy. They will all laugh at you."

In deep dejection he turned homewards, closed his house and wandered away towards the North. He meant to go on wandering, until fate brought him a wife. So he travelled on day after day, and when the cart-drivers he met on the road asked him, "Where are you going?" he would answer, "I don't know;" upon which they laughed and thought he was a bit cracked. But his thought was only, "Laugh away!" On no account would he tell every goose on the high-road that he was going northwards in search of a wife.

One day he saw a beautiful lake lying some distance off from the high-road, very inviting looking with its border of shady trees. He went towards it, and was just about to stretch himself out comfortably upon its banks, when he heard a shriek, and, looking round, saw a girl fall from a tree. He sprang swiftly to her assistance, but her injury was nothing worse than a sprained ankle. Nala sat down beside the girl, and waited till she had finished crying, for she carried on, not as if she had sprained an ankle, but as if she had broken both her legs.

When at last she grew quiet, she began to wonder that Nala never spoke a word.

"Why don't you say something? Do you know how I got up this tree?" she said.

"No."

"Well, ask!"

"I may not ask. It is a vow."

"Dear me! What a bad vow!" said the girl, pityingly. "What do you do then, when you lose your way and don't know how to find it again?"

"It is not like that; it is only that I may not ask a *woman* anything."

"Oh, is that it?" she laughed. "Well, since you may not ask, I will tell you myself how I got up the tree. But what is your name?"

"I am called Nala."

"And I am called Katha. You mustn't think that is my right name, but that is what people call me, so you may call me that too. You see, the village folk say that if a maiden climbs up this tree in the daytime, and eats all the berries, without being seen by a man —you must know that many people bathe here—the first young man she afterwards meets is her future husband. If, however, she is surprised in the act by any one, then it is all over. The worst of it is that I had just picked the last berry, and my stomach was as full as a barrel, when up you came and spoiled everything. As I caught sight of you, I got frightened, made a misstep, and tumbled down."

"I'm awfully sorry," said Nala, and looked at her with much concern. "But what a stupid I am!" he suddenly exclaimed, striking himself on the brow. "I didn't see you on the tree at all; I only saw you when you fell."

"Really? Are you quite sure?"

"Quite sure! You can depend on that. Your heel was at least a hand-breadth from the tree when I saw you."

"Did I fall head over heels, Nala?"

"Very likely, Katha."

"Did I look very foolish as I was falling down?"

Nala reflected, while she scrutinised him keenly. "Try to remember!" she urged him.

"Really I don't know. You came down so fast."

"Did you ever before see a girl fall from a tree?"

"Never in my life."

After a pause she began, "If you are sure, Nala, that my heel was already out of the tree, everything may still be all right. But what a stupid I am!" she suddenly exclaimed, striking herself on the brow. "If you haven't seen me on the tree, then——" She halted.

"Indeed, Katha, you are right." He also halted.

"I must go home now," she said, and made to rise. But she had forgotten her hurt ankle, and gave a loud cry of pain.

"Dear me! How shall I ever get home?" she wailed.

"I will carry you," he said resolutely.

She laughed again. "It is much too far. But I'll tell you what: just carry me as far as the high-road. There I will wait till a cart comes along and gives me a lift."

So Nala took her up in his arms to carry her to the high-road. She leant away from him.

"Put your arm round my neck," he said, "I can't carry you that way."

Then she put her left arm round his neck, and just because she was now in such a position, she said, "Nala, I love you."

"Then you can become my wife, Katha," Nala quickly cried.

"Can I really?" she retorted pertly; "there are more than you that are courting me."

"I only thought . . . because you were up in the tree," said Nala, dejectedly.

"Oh, that was only a girl's prank," she answered down to him. "All the girls in the village do the same. You mustn't think that everything is quite settled for you because you saw me fall from the tree."

"All the same, I am your husband to be," persisted Nala.

"Yes, if I will have you."

"But you have already said that you love me."

"That doesn't matter. How can I become your wife if you don't ask me?"

"But I can't ask any woman, Katha."

"And when you are married will you never ask your wife if she still loves you?"

"I must not, Katha."

"Nala," she said, and clasped her arms a trifle tighter round his neck, "are you not tired now?"

"Not in the least," he said brightly, and gave her a slight toss by way of confirmation.

She laughed with pleasure and said, "Nala, I can't really let you off from the question. But if you can't put it at all, then I will let you do something else in its place. If you will carry me from here to my village, I will be your wife without any asking, and I'll give you just the very sweetest betrothal kiss when we get there. If on the way you even only ask if you may put me down, then you have lost the bargain. If I get too heavy for you, you have only to say: 'Katha, will you become my wife?' and everything is all right."

They had now reached the high-road. Nala was a sturdy fellow. He thought, "I can easily do it. From now on I may wander till I am old and grey if I don't succeed here." He considered women the rarest articles in the world. So he said—

"All right! Katha; that's a bargain. I am to carry you right into the village."

"No! what are you thinking of? Only as far as the Buddha image. I will point it out to you directly. There is only one."

"Good! But I also have my conditions."

"What are they like?"

"First of all, allow me to put you down here just once."

"That you may do, Nala."

He let her slip down carefully on to the grass.

"Secondly, you must hold on to me quite tight, so as to make it easier for me."

"I will do that too, Nala."

"And, thirdly, you mustn't say a single word to me on the way. If you only let out a single sound, you have lost and I have won."

"I promise you on my sacred word."

Nala thought that he had now provided well for everything. One thing only he had forgotten to ascertain, about how far it was to her village.

When he was thoroughly rested, he took her up again in his arms, as one might take a child. True to her promise, she snuggled up so close to him, that her firm round bosom lay full on his breast.

"Will that do?" she asked, "but these words don't count yet, for you haven't begun to walk."

"Yes, that will do," he said, with strained voice; "I am starting now."

With that he began to step out. He felt as if he would have liked to journey thus all his life with such a burden in his arms. He distinctly heard the little heart give beat after beat; he felt the rise and fall of the little body, and her gentle breathing fell on his cheek like a cooling breeze. He thought he had never felt so happy in all his life. In silent bliss he walked along. "Why ever did the Exalted One teach, 'To whom not anything is dear—to him not anything is grievous?'" he thought. "What grief for me can grow out of this dear one?" Never was vow in greater danger of being broken.

It was now early afternoon and the sun shone mercilessly hot. Nala had scarcely gone a few hundred paces when he found himself extremely hot and thirsty, but he still strode valiantly along. The girl lay silent on his breast. Ever slower became his steps, ever stronger the temptation to put the little question, which at one stroke would give him everything and take only one thing from him—his vow.

He waited quietly to see if Katha would not, perhaps, forget herself and say something, such as, "Just look at that beautiful bird, Nala!" or, "There's a stone, Nala! Take care!" or, "There is a nice shady place! Go there, Nala!" But nothing of the kind happened. She was as dumb as a stone.

He began to pant. The perspiration ran down his purple face. The living body in his arms, but lately bliss incorporate, had now become as lead for him, and heated him most unbearably. From time to time he shifted his burden a little in order to enjoy a moment's freedom from her breast. "How obstinate the woman is!" he thought.

She on her part felt quite comfortable and calculated in this wise: "If he is such a stubborn fellow that he would rather faint with exhaustion than give up his silly vow, I must cure him of his obstinacy in good time. If I give in to-day, I must always give in. Besides, what have I to lose? If he puts me down, I have won. If he carries me to the end, well—I haven't lost anything." So, perfectly at her ease, she allowed herself to be rocked up and down, and listened to Nala's panting with the same interest as that with which a sailor might listen to the creaking of his ship.

But, as the panting became ever more painful, amounting almost to a groan; as the footsteps became ever more tottering, she turned her head anxiously and looked into Nala's face. It had become pale; the veins stood out, thick as her fingers, on neck and temples, and the eyes appeared ready to start from their sockets.

Nala noticed the movement and thought, "Thank Heaven! At last! Now she is going to say, 'Enough! That will do.'"

And really, when she looked down into the strange face of the man she was alarmed; but she tightened her lips, which meant, "If he holds to his vow, I hold to mine."

Nala thought, "How merciless the woman is!" He made a last effort. At a turn in the road the Buddha image beckoned. With trembling knees, ready to drop with fatigue, he laid his burden down on the plinth of the image.

The girl immediately spread out her arms lovingly and pursed up her mouth for the betrothal kiss. Nala, however, sighed twice, deeply and long, as if the full heart would free itself of something that weighed upon it: then he said—

"Wait a bit, Katha!"

With that he began to wipe the perspiration from him with the back of his hand. But the back of a hand was of little good to that flood! Then he took his pocket-handkerchief, then the sleeve of his white jacket, and finally, the end of his loin-cloth. He did not hurry; indeed, it almost looked as if he found a deliberate pleasure in taking his time, and the stone Buddha looked down on him and smiled. Meanwhile, the girl sat firmly on the pedestal looking like one who would like to sneeze and cannot, or like one whose mouth is full of water and yet dares not spit it out.

When at last Nala was ready, he said affably—

"Maiden, pardon me! It has come to me on the way, that your heel was still in the tree when I saw you falling down, so you will have to go back and eat berries again." Which said, he wheeled round, and went full speed back home.

Arrived there, he looked down once more upon the broad plain at his feet, on which the distant hillocks seemed like ships upon an ocean, and the streams like veins of silver; and every day he beheld the great sun rise in the east and go down in the west. And because he lived there, in serene solitude, year after year, he finally came to acquire the reputation of being a sage; indeed, a saint. And when any one—sufferers, burdened ones—come to him and ask him, "Father, how have you attained this state of quiet serenity?" he usually answers, "To whom not anything is dear—to him not anything is grievous!" And if his visitor is a man, he adds, "Never put a question to a woman!"

Thus did Nala become increasingly famous for wisdom and sanctity. And to whomsoever life has become a painful thing, he needs only to go and see if Nala is still alive; for his motto is a good motto.

RENUNCIATION

IN the town of Akyab in Burma there lived a man named Maung Hpay, who was a Burmese judge of the township and first in rank after the English Chief Magistrate. He was everywhere held in the highest esteem, so that people, when they met him, always bowed deeply and said : " How do you do, Maung Hpay ? "

This man had a pretty wife, a little son, a fine house, a fair portion of money and property, and all the comfort and content which the possession of these things is supposed to bestow. In addition, he had hopes, which he kept quietly to himself, of one day becoming a judge in Rangoon City.

" That is something different from Akyab, and if then I have a praying-hall built up on the platform of Shwè Dagon Pagoda, with an inscription in large gold letters upon it: 'Erected by Maung Hpay, Chief Magistrate, at an expenditure of so many rupees'—why, that would be doing something worth while! Then, my little son is growing up. He is scarcely two years old yet, but already he promises well. He will be clever, enter government service, and marry a rich wife. And if my wife should yet present me with a little daughter, as beautiful as herself, what a fine match she might make!" In such foolish fashion as this did Maung Hpay think things over, as he sat of an evening on his veranda smoking his after-dinner cheroot.

One morning this Maung Hpay sat at breakfast in the house. The evening before he had eaten somewhat too freely of durians, and in consequence had slept rather badly. He had waked up feeling out of sorts and heavy of head, and now sat down absent-mindedly to the business of eating, which with him was usually a very important business indeed.

For dessert there were mangoes. As he bit, unthinking, into one, his teeth encountered its hard, stony core. He experienced a sudden sharp pain, and spat out of his mouth a piece of tooth that had been broken off. The pain soon passed away, but Maung Hpay was now in quite a different mood from before. He held the morsel of bony substance in his hand, and said gravely and thoughtfully: "So passes away our body. What is this but a kind of dying? We die daily and hourly and take no heed. What a wretched thing is this body of ours!"

Now, Maung Hpay was also a school-manager, and on this very day he purposed paying a visit to the Girls' School, which stood close by the little Chinese Temple. His mind occupied by these and similar reflections, he left his house and entered the school building. The mistress received him with the greatest respect, and he passed through the different rooms, here and there putting a question, and in one of the lower classes asked the teacher for some test of the progress made by her little pupils.

The teacher began: "Why are you born?"

"That we may die," rang back the answer from thirty fresh, child throats.

Maung Hpay felt as if the walls around him were alive and were flinging at him this "That we may die." He heard nothing of what followed; he stared straight before him as if at the source of the voice.

He scarcely noticed when the lesson ended and the teacher turned towards him. His brain seemed to him to be a gong that went on reverberating with this "That we may die." Usually, at the end of the inspection he would pass a joke or two with the teachers, and pat some of the children on the head by way of approval of their work, but to-day there was nothing of this. He left the building without a single word, so that the teachers could not help looking after him in perplexity. Once he was outside the building, something cried within him: "O Thou lotus-enthroned One, how truly, how clearly, in Thy boundless compassion, hast Thou laid down for us everything that we need to know, and—wretch that I am!—how have I paid heed to it? For five and thirty years, now, have I been hastening towards death, and at every moment of that time have been in danger of meeting Him face to face! and what, up till now, have I done to prepare myself beforehand for such an encounter? Oh how foolish we men are! We torment ourselves over this thing, and worry ourselves about some other thing, but of that in regard to which we ought continually to be on the watch, we simply never think at all. Woe is me! When will it be otherwise? When? To-day, fool! Now! Here on this very spot that my foot even now treads." Unconsciously he lengthened his steps and strode swiftly along.

At this moment a beggar, squatting on the ground, begged an alms of him. In the tumult of his emotion, he felt in his pocket, and flung his well-furnished purse with its entire contents into the beggar's lap.

"Before all things, giving! Giving is the first rung on the ladder. No one can reach the higher rungs who has not first trodden the lower," thought Maung Hpay as he passed on his way. This morning the great

Transiency-idea and, with it, the cognition, "It is wiser to be good than to be bad!" had taken root in Maung Hpay's heart, but this root can never again be torn up. However slowly it may sprout and grow, still it does sprout and grow, until finally the blossom and, following the blossom, the fruit appears. Maung Hpay had begun his great renunciation.

Maung Hpay's wife quickly noticed that in more than one respect her husband had become quite another man. She pondered much and often over what the reason might be, but all without success. She knew of nothing for which she herself could be to blame. There had been no dispute between them. Husband and wife had always had a fond regard for one another, and this fond regard had thrown up round them a sort of rampart, as it were, which shut them off from the rest of the world. To Maung Hpay care had always meant care for his own family alone. All outside it were to him strangers and aliens. So it had been up till now. What then did all this extravagant giving mean? Her husband appeared to her to be putting everybody on the same level in his regard as his own wife and child. What a mistaken way of looking at things! Why has nature drawn us closer to one than to another? Obviously that we may care for that one more than for others.

One day she spoke to him. "You give and give, and never appear to bethink you that you have a little son. What will become of him if you give everything away to strangers? And who knows," she proceeded significantly, "whether Kamma may not yet send us a little daughter. Where is her dowry to come from?"

"Wife, Kamma will never send us another child."

The woman held her peace. She saw what her husband meant. She thought: "Holy men belong to the monastery. Whoever is in life must live."

So passed the better part of a year. Maung Hpay lived "restrained of body, restrained of speech, restrained of mind," and gave lavishly, so that all the needy of

Akyab swarmed round him like flies round a pot of honey, and his worldly wealth more and more melted away.

One day a serious case came before the courts for trial; a native Burman had murdered his wife. The English Chief Magistrate was out in the district upon a lengthy tour, and Maung Hpay had to preside over the trial.

The facts of the case were briefly these:

The accused, a man fifty-two years of age and a cripple from his birth—he had come into the world with a shapeless stump where his right hand should have been—had married about a year before. His wife was seventeen years of age. One night, out of jealousy, he had murdered her in her sleep.

As soon as the man was brought before him, Maung Hpay began—

"Speak! Do you admit having killed your wife named so and so?"

"Yes, sir."

"Why didst thou do it? Why didst thou so give way to rage against thine own self unhappy that thou art, here and hereafter?"

"Yes, sir, I have given way to rage against myself, unhappy that I am, here and hereafter. But what else could I do? Could you stand it if your wife became set against you and another kissed and fondled her?"

Here the mother of the murdered woman, who also had been summoned to court, interrupted him with a cry:

"You grey-haired wretch! You old libertine! Can you wonder that things have so happened with you? What did you take a wife of sixteen for? Day and night did you plague my poor child with your jealous ways, while she was still a faithful wife to you."

The veins swelled on the man's brow. He gave the old woman a terrible look.

"Accursed match-maker, did you not sell me your daughter for money?"

Maung Hpay ordered silence.

"Man, tell me how it all happened," he said, turning to the accused.

The accused began, "See, sir, thus was

I born!" With that, he stretched out the stump of his arm towards the judge. "My father was shot before my birth. My mother died before I had even learned to say 'Mother.' As long as I can remember I have lived by begging. What could I work at? You must know that I am not only a cripple, but also burdened with an illness. People say that it is the evil Nats that torment me; for I am dragged to the ground without my being able to prevent it, and I strike and kick all round me like a madman.

"One day, as I was going as usual to my place at the great pagoda, I was attacked by the Nats right in front of this woman's stall," and he pointed to the murdered woman's mother.

"You must know, sir," the woman again interrupted, "I deal in fruit, and have earned my bread in an honourable way all my days, and have given two annas every week for the new image of the Buddha."

Maung Hpay signed to her to be quiet, and the cripple went on:

"As I lay on the ground, this woman's daughter thought, 'It might be a good thing if I did a charitable deed.' Whereupon she came over to me and helped me up. As she did so, my shoulder came into contact with her bosom. This shoulder, sir," he repeated, at the same time slightly raising his left shoulder. "That, sir, was my evil destiny."

"Why was it thy evil destiny?" asked Maung Hpay.

"Only think of it, sir! I was almost fifty years of age, and, as true as I'm standing here before you, I had never yet even touched a woman's breast."

The woman opposite laughed maliciously. The man did not appear to notice it. He looked like one lit up from within by some fiery glow.

"It was a stroke of destiny, sir. This was the beginning of all my misfortune. Up till then I had lived happily. The beggar has the best of it, sir."

Maung Hpay nodded.

"Everything was different now. I was

no longer content to get my daily bread by begging. I kept thinking, 'What's the use?' And so things went for a year."

"Every day he ran past our stall and stared at my daughter," the woman screamed out again.

"It is true. I could not help it. But my greatest misfortune was still to come. One day I was sitting in my place, when one came past from whom I begged for a pice. He threw a heavy purse down to me. I open!—I count!—Sir, two hundred and fifty rupees! Cursed be the money! I remain sitting; I do not dare to move. I think: 'If I stir, it will all disappear.' I think: 'He will come back again and take it away.' Nothing of the sort happened. I had two hundred and fifty rupees, sir, really and truly, all my own. I got up and went straight to that woman there—what else should I do?—and said, 'I will give you a hundred rupees. Give me your daughter for my wife.'"

"You lying rascal! It was fifty rupees that you offered. I had to squeeze rupee after rupee out of you."

"Woman," said Maung Hpay, "why dost thou cry abroad thine own infamy?"

"Am I not a widow, sir? Do I not give two annas every week for the new image of the Buddha? Where is everything to come from? It is the custom with us."

"Very well; that will do. Prisoner, proceed."

"Sir, I gave a hundred rupees to the old woman, and presented the daughter with a golden bracelet. Three days later we were married."

"Then she was fond of you?" Maung Hpay asked.

"Sir, he captivated my poor child with his gold. Only think! A bracelet as heavy as a chain!"

"Was she fond of you, then?" Maung Hpay again asked.

"Sir, she became my wife of her own free will."

"Did you not see that she was too young for you?"

"Sir, all I wanted was a wife. It never came into my head that I might look round for some one else. It was like a stroke of destiny. I could not think of anything else."

"Well, what next?"

"Perhaps all might yet have been well. You can imagine how I prized her. I prized her like a pearl from India, like a diamond from the mine."

"Yes, he would like to have shut her up in a box and never shown her to any one," sneered the woman.

"With some of the money we began a small business. Everything went well, and then one day this man with the long hair and the almond eyes came. He has now gone away to Moulmein or somewhere. He came one day and spoke to her. I said, 'Why do you talk so long with him?' She says, 'Am I not to dare speak any more to anybody, now that I have married so high?'"

"He is a relative of my dead husband's," the woman again broke in. "They have known one another from childhood up. He had been four years in Bangkok, and had only just come back. What of it, sir, if they did speak a long time to one another? My daughter told me all about it. My daughter was virtue itself. His madness is to blame for everything."

"So you admit that your daughter has broken faith with the prisoner here?" Maung Hpay asked.

"Sir, what else can a poor woman do but turn to a stranger, when her own husband torments her day and night?"

"Go on, prisoner!"

"Sir," he said moodily, "there is not much more to tell. One day I came upon the two of them unawares in this woman's house. I acted as though I had not noticed anything; otherwise I knew that she would have run away from me before the night."

"Why did you not let the unfaithful wife run away?"

"How, sir?" The man looked at Maung Hpay in astonishment. "Let her run away! My wife! She would then have taken the other."

"Well, what of it? She was an unfaithful wife."

"Quite true, sir. But just think; I was fifty years old before I got a wife, and now was I to give her to another?"

"You have not got her now."

"True, sir. But still I could not give her to another."

Maung Hpay was silent a little space, and then said—

"Tell us the end."

"The end, sir, was this. I dissembled until night came. This night she was pleasant with me as she had only been during the first days of our married life. But I kept still. Then she said, 'I believe you think there is something between that man and me.' So I was obliged to dissemble yet more, and so everything happened. . . . When I saw that she was asleep, I took a dagger, and gently drew apart her bosom wrapper, so that her breast lay bare, and twice approached the point to within a hair's breadth of the place where I meant to stab her. Then, however, I thought, 'What a pity!' What happened next or how it happened I do not myself know, but suddenly I had caught her by the throat and strangled her."

"With one hand?"

"Yes, sir, with one hand. I don't know myself how it was possible. She scarcely moved. I only kept squeezing until she lay quite still. I could not then give her to another."

Here the woman broke into a howl half-way between rage and grief. She made as if she would fling herself upon the murderer. A warder held her back.

Maung Hpay sat reflecting. He appeared to be thinking the whole affair over. At last he began—

"It is good for thee, both here and hereafter, that thou confessest all. Give now all respect to the truth. If thou liest, thou liest to thyself, not to us. Those two hundred and fifty rupees—pay attention!—you stole them?"

"Sir," said the accused vehemently, "by the bones of my mother, I have never yet stolen as much as a grain of rice. . . . I can see it all yet as if it were only yesterday. He was a Burman, but a man of position. He carried his head well up. I did not know if it would be any use begging from him. I think he came out of the school close to the Chinese Temple."

Maung Hpay started. His eyes, which had hitherto been directed scrutinisingly towards the prisoner, changed their expression, as if turned upon an object in their immediate neighbourhood. A secret something seemed to pass from him over to the other. The eyes of the prisoner also changed their expression. He stood suddenly stricken dumb. It was like the moment between lightning-flash and thunder-clap. Then he said quite quietly—

"Sir, you are the man. Cursed be your gift."

A death-like stillness followed. Maung Hpay pulled himself together and ordered the accused and the woman to be led away. The case must now be put to the jury and judgment pronounced—here a mere formality. According to the law of the land, there was no alternative but the death sentence. Maung Hpay, however, abruptly declared the sitting closed, and left the court chamber. Everything in him raged and whirled, but always round one fixed point: "I have no right to condemn this man to death. The law, however, commands it. How can you be a judge, Maung Hpay, if you do not carry out the law? Then I must give up this post. Are men justified at all in sitting in judgment upon others? But what have men in general to do with me? The question here is: 'Am I justified in sitting in judgment upon others?' I must answer, 'No!' My only duty day and night is to sit in judgment upon myself."

By this time Maung Hpay arrived at his house, and said to his wife—

"Wife, I have to-day resigned my post as judge. I cannot be a judge any longer."

"Why?" she asked.

"I have no right to judge others."

"Those worse than you are still judges."

"What has that to do with me? May

they also see when they are ready for seeing!"

"Husband," began the wife again, "whether you are right or no in being a judge—that I cannot say. But this I can say—that you have taken upon you the duty of supporting wife and child. How can we live if you no longer hold any post? Beggars have eaten up your substance."

"Wife, how we shall live we shall know when it gets as far as that. We have our little property in the country."

"Oh yes, our little property in the country! Will you yourself buckle down to hoeing and watering like any day-labourer? And what do you expect to get out of our property? Rice to keep us from starving!"

Maung Hpay was silent, but that same day he sent in his resignation to the government, giving, however, no reason for his sudden resolve.

After some time, an English official appeared at his house, to ask him why he was leaving the service, for it was the rule that officers of the government who gave up their posts by reason of old age or sickness should receive a year's salary.

Maung Hpay answered the question without any beating about the bush.

"I cannot serve as judge any longer."

"Why not?" asked the other in astonishment.

"I have no right to sit in judgment upon another."

The stranger looked at him suspiciously. Was the man in his sane senses?

"Maung Hpay," he began, "you are a servant of this State. You have eaten its bread for years, and on your part have sworn to be faithful to it. But is that being faithful to it, to refuse to carry out those laws which it finds necessary to its own wellbeing?"

"The State will find others to look after its wellbeing. To be true to one's self is of more importance than to be true to the State. To be true to one's self—that is Truth. Truth first; the State afterwards."

"To what extent do you violate Truth, when, according to your best conscience and knowledge, you preside in court?"

"Whoso is true knows: 'Day and night I must sit in judgment upon myself.'"

"Oh, one cannot take such things so seriously."

"My dear sir, what in all the world is serious, if that is not? What lies closer to us than our own wellbeing? If I am really friends with myself, how can I venture to take the life of another man?"

"Oh," replied the other, "I see; you have gone over to the new sect which reprehends all shedding of blood and holds that war is immoral. One cannot take things so seriously as all that and translate them into actual practice. Otherwise one would make one's self quite useless in the world. These things are all right to talk about after dinner over a cigar. After all, the middle way is always the safest. All sectarianism is dangerous."

"I belong to the sect of those who hold it to be more sensible and more profitable to be good than to be bad. One, however, can only be good when one is true."

"I fear you will derive but little profit out of this affair."

"It all depends upon how you look at it."

The official shrugged his shoulders and went away. Maung Hpay received his dismissal without any year's salary.

They were now obliged to leave their beautiful house in the town, with its broad veranda, its spacious apartments and roomy compound, and betake themselves to the little house which stood on Maung Hpay's paddy land and belonged to himself.

As they left the town, the wife threw her arms round her little son, and said, weeping—

"Woe is thine, my poor child!" She would have liked to add, "It is all the fault of thy father;" but she was afraid.

Since, however, she could not entirely choke down her feelings, she said spitefully to Maung Hpay—

"The beggars and idlers will have to get

along without you now, and they will still live."

"Wife," he replied, "I did not give to beggars and idlers; I gave to myself."

Again the wife began to cry bitterly, and continued crying without intermission the whole way.

"Wife," at last Maung Hpay said, "do be quiet! What will people think?"

"Is it you that say, 'What will people think?' You!" She burst out into a scornful laugh, and then again sobbed as if her heart would break.

Maung Hpay lost patience now. Somewhat harshly he gripped her by the arm.

"Be still with your crying, I tell you!"

At the pressure of his hand she started. For a moment she looked at him without a word, then she turned round and sat down by the side of the road, covering her face with her hands. The child seated itself near her. It began to pick the flowers round about and to lay them one after the other in her lap. At the same time, in childish roguery, it tried to peer from below between the closed fingers that concealed its mother's face. It thought she was playing with it. For a moment Maung Hpay stood irresolute. Then he suddenly seized his little son's hand and said—

"Come, my child, we will go on."

But his hand did not feel the same as usual and his voice was strange.

The child began to cry and pressed up to its mother who, fondling it, took it on to her lap.

A strange icy feeling crept over Maung Hpay's heart. He thought, "Even this cannot stand the test. Nothing can be depended on."

Suddenly his wife looked up and saw him, as if in thought. Hastily she got up, pushed the child before her and said—

"Go, my child, go to your father. We will all go."

Maung Hpay gently took his son's little hand in his own, and in silence they went to their new home.

It was just at the season of the paddy planting. Without any ceremony Maung

Hpay put himself to the work. One single day-labourer was all the help he had. Whilst he worked outside in the field, his wife looked after the house and Maung Hpay thought—

"When did I ever live as happily as I do now? Whoever lives by the soil, lives best. How happy am I that I have come back to the soil!"

And Maung Hpay would indeed have been still happier, if he had not been obliged to see day after day the dull, sad expression of his wife's countenance. When, however, the shining green of the young paddy plants covered his field, he scarcely noticed any longer his wife's looks. It was so beautiful to look at the paddy growing.

"How pure! How full of innocence!" he thought. "Here is security."

But Maung Hpay's joy was not to be of long duration. In place of the rain-bringing sea-wind, there came the scorching land-wind that burnt up the field, and their store was scarcely sufficient to keep them alive till next harvest time. Everything that was still left of their old property had to be sold bit by bit, and they fell into the greatest poverty. And the hot winds not only brought bad harvests but diseases as well. Fever was very prevalent, and Maung Hpay and his wife felt weak and wretched.

One morning the child refused its food. By midday it lay in a high fever. At night it seemed as if it could not live any longer. The mother knelt in despair by the bed-side, while Maung Hpay looked in dumb anguish at the heaving breast and the wandering eyes. They both knew that it was the worst kind of fever, the fever that often kills in one day. Of their neighbours round scarcely one had recovered who had been attacked by it.

At last the woman said, "If we could only get an English doctor. But where are we to get the money?" she added bitterly. "There isn't a copper coin in the whole house."

Maung Hpay was silent.

After a while she began again, "If we only had some quinine. They give nothing but quinine, but in the town they say that it cures."

Maung Hpay still kept silence, but suddenly he began—

"I will see whether I can get any money."

"Where will you get any money? All our goods are gone. We have parted with the last bit, as you well know. Or perhaps you do not know that I lately put away the yellow silk jacket with the fancy work on it? That was the last thing of all. No one in the town any longer looks at you, and I haven't a relative in the world."

She appeared to be on the point of breaking into tears again, but a glance at the child restrained her.

"Then I must beg now."

The wife bowed over her child and answered nothing. Maung Hpay left the house silently. He himself was not very clear in his mind as to what he was going to do. One thing only was clear to him—that he could not allow his child to perish simply for lack of a couple of doses of quinine.

Driven by this thought he flung forth. But how to get the money? The more he reflected on that, the slower became his steps. Now he was in the town. What to do? What to do? To beg one of his old acquaintances for half a rupee? Impossible! Maung Hpay, the late Chief Magistrate, resolved to beg at the street corner. He drew the outer garment, as worn by the country people, well over his head, and sat himself down upon the lowest step of a pagoda where all the beggars sat.

For a few moments he felt at peace as he sat upon the stone, but immediately he began to reflect—

"That I should be sitting here in the steeet, begging a couple of annas for my child, must be owing to some error in my life's sum. Unless I can find out this error and put it right, the further I count, the greater it will become. Had I given less, had I kept my post, I would not need to be sitting here now. But I would have been neglecting my own real wellbeing. Would it have been right to give up one's self merely to maintain one's wife and child in comfort? But whoso has once got a wife and a child must also take care of them."

Maung Hpay groaned. His thoughts lay heavy upon him like enormous blocks of stone. He knew not how to escape. He scarcely thought now of the object of his sitting here on the pagoda steps. Suddenly something fell into his lap. He started with fright. It was a copper coin. He glanced at the giver, and saw a wealthy-looking lady who was taking from her purse and giving to every beggar that squatted upon the steps. The thought came to him: "Speak to this one, she will give you something more." But an unconquerable timidity kept his mouth closed. "How difficult it is to beg!" he thought, and then, "It is difficult because you have not learnt it." When the lady came back—then he would speak to her. He waited for over an hour but she did not come. Finally, he rose and went on to the platform where the worshippers kneel. She was not there. She had left the pagoda by the flight of steps on the other side of the platform, apparently that she might be able to give also to the beggars who sat there. He squatted down again in his old place, but had little hope. A nameless terror came over him. It seemed to him as if he already saw his dead child lying on the bed before him. What to do? What to do? In despair he wrung his hands and looked wildly round him. As he did so, his eye met that of another beggar crouched near him. He was an old grey-haired man. He began to speak.

"I have never seen you here before. Where did you use to sit?"

"Nowhere," Maung Hpay said shortly.

"But you must have sat somewhere?"

"No."

Maung Hpay kept his eyes fixed on the ground.

"Oh, the beginning," said the old beggar, nodding his head as if in thought. "You see," he went on, prattling as the old will prattle, "in no calling is the beginning so difficult as in this."

"Do you call begging also a 'calling'?" said Maung Hpay. He did not himself know why he answered; apparently it was only to find some relief from his gnawing pain.

"Of course it is a calling. Begging requires to be learnt."

Maung Hpay groaned.

The old man went on: "When I began some ten or more years ago, I understood nothing about begging. I thought the more urgently one begs the more one gets. I had to save myself and my sick wife from starvation. I myself was ill, you must know—wounded, could not work. But the more I begged the more I was repulsed. My wife slowly starved to death because I did not understand begging. So it is in the big towns. Nobody starves in the country. I can speak about it now like this because I know that to die is the lot of man. What is subject to death is as good as dead already. We can't help it. But when my wife was dead I sat down at a street corner and thought: 'Here, in the eyes of everybody I will starve to death. Even if you were now to give to me, I would not take.' But now behold! one coin after another fell into my lap, and in the evening I was able to get a good meal. It was, as it were, the funeral feast. Since then I never again went hungry. That is how it is in begging. You must not want anything, and then they give. You give me nothing?—very well; I am prepared to starve."

Maung Hpay groaned aloud. He had heard but little of the old man's talk; his ears were filled with the groaning of his child. He found it impossible to sit a moment longer doing nothing. He sprang up. The sun was going down, and he held in his hand nothing but one copper coin. Something must be done. He wanted to go and beg from some one whom he knew. He wanted—he no longer rightly knew what. He began to run. At the street corner, right in front of him, he saw a money-changer crouching before his open box of piled-up rolls of money. It all came over him like a vertigo. For a brief moment all thought forsook him. . . .

"Stop the thief!" was the cry he heard behind him.

He had only run a few steps when he was caught, and the hand that held the money was forced to relax its convulsive clutch on the copper coins. Every one was beside himself. Such a thing had never happened before. To rob a money-changer of his money on the open street! Maung Hpay would have been beaten almost to death if some one had not shouted out, "Hold! that is Maung Hpay who gave to the poor." Meanwhile, a policeman came up and took him away to the station.

He was led before the inspector, a dignified but still fairly young Burman in European dress. He scarcely looked up from his desk.

"What is it?" he asked over his shoulder.

The man told him.

"Extraordinary!" He turned round to look at the criminal.

Maung Hpay stood, pale as death, staring vacantly before him. The other looked fixedly at him, got up quickly, and stepped over to him.

"In Heaven's name, Maung Hpay, is it you?" he began in English.

Maung Hpay awoke as if out of stupor.

Before him stood an acquaintance of his early days, a kindly-disposed acquaintance, not strictly a friend. Maung Hpay had really never had any friends.

The inspector signed to the officer, who immediately took his departure.

"Sit down. Tell me. What has happened?"

Maung Hpay collapsed into the proffered seat and buried his face in his hands. He groaned as one groans who cannot quite master a frightful physical pain. The other waited patiently a while; then he began again in Burmese: "I beg you, Maung Hpay; do tell me!" Then Maung Hpay told how all had happened.

The other listened in silence. One could read pity in his expression. As soon, however, as the narrative was ended, he said—

"Maung Hpay, a man with a wife and child ought not to behave like this. But now is not the time for reproaches, your child must have immediate help. You yourself cannot go; you see I must detain you here, but I will do all in my power to secure your being set free to-morrow. I myself will get the quinine and take it to the child. I know the place where you live. It is just coming on for my time to be relieved from duty. How fortunate that you came here before I went off!"

Maung Hpay wished to thank him. The other stopped him.

"Never mind, it is nothing! I must now have you put in a cell, but don't be down-hearted; you will be home again by to-morrow."

Dull and stupid, Maung Hpay allowed himself to be led down to a dark cell. His thoughts roved from this to that. Wife and child also were down there, but this he did not see quite clearly; his brain refused to think anything out. Only one thing held his mind: "Whether there were in this dark hole rats or snakes or other reptiles?" He had always had an inexplicable horror of all such things. Suddenly it seemed to him that the old man on the pagoda steps again sat near him. He was now fleshless, like a death's head, and grinned horribly at him.

Maung Hpay involuntarily glanced sideways into the darkness. White mists, as it were, floated past his over-strained retina. He shut his eyes and sank his head low upon his breast.

Then everything that the old man had said returned to his recollection. How wonderful! He did not really know that he had heard it all, yet now every word of it came back to him. "You must not want anything, and then they give."

Yes, yes, one must abandon in order to possess, abandon everything, everything. And when one also abandons his very self, then one possesses all. "Maung Hpay, a man with a wife and child ought not to behave like this," he again heard sounding in his ears. "Alas! Alas! Where, where was the mistake in my reckoning?"

It was not until the afternoon of the next day that Maung Hpay was released from custody. It was made out that he had acted as he did in a fit of temporary mental alienation.

He glanced timidly round as he stepped

out into the street. His face had taken on a strange, wild look in the course of this one night. He felt as if everybody must be looking at him. As if pursued, he hurried through the streets, not drawn by longing but driven by the thought, "They are looking at you." Only when he had come close to his hut did the thought occur to him, "What shall I find here?" Everything about the house was quiet. "The child is dead already," he thought, and did not wince as he thought it.

Like a worn-out old man he stepped inside. There sat his wife in the act of giving the child some rice porridge. For a moment he stood staring in astonishment, saying nothing. Then his wife jumped up with the child in her arm and stepped swiftly up to him. She scarcely seemed to feel the weight of the child.

"Oh, are you back again? What trouble I have had! By evening I thought all was over. Then your friend Maung Tok came. He brought the quinine—Oh, much more than was needed. But only think! Then he went away and came back again with an English doctor. They both came in a carriage. He came in here like Mahadeva himself and the doctor after him. What a man!" She fondled the child. "My sweet little darling!" she said lovingly. Her face glowed: Maung Hpay had not seen his wife look so young and so beautiful for many a long day.

He answered nothing; he did not even fondle his child that had been saved. Bitterness reigned in his heart. At least Maung Hpay thought so. In truth it was the feeling of freeing himself, which at the first taste is always bitter as wormwood. It was to him as if out of this hut there came an emanation that struck against him, kept him off and sought to drive him away. For a moment he quivered with the thought, "Down at the pagoda would have been better than this."

But now the child began to cry; it wanted the remainder of the rice porridge. The wife returned to her seat; Maung Hpay followed. As she fed the child she began again—

"You see, it went away as quickly as it came. He is very weak now. He cannot stand, but he is well."

She spoke so briskly and brightly that Maung Hpay again was astonished.

"Wife," he at last said, vexed at his own silence, "I am tired out, I must sleep."

With that he lay down on his bed and turned his face to the wall. Ere he fell asleep, he heard his wife lay the child beside him and hum a lullaby over it. What a long time it was since last she had sung!

When next he woke it was night; the moon shone brightly into the room. His wife lay there with the child in her arms, its little hands clasping one another round her neck.

Maung Hpay sat up and looked round him. How clear and cold was this moonlight, bright as day but yet so different. It was to him as if now for the first time he saw things in reality, as if that delusive glamour with which the sunlight surrounds everything had been chased away. Singular! Had he then never seen his home, his wife, his child by moonlight before? It all looked foreign to him. What mattered to him the two who lay there fondly clasping one another? There was no room there for a third. He smiled a little. Perhaps there *was* room for a third. He rose softly, and, without once looking back at wife or child, he left his house for ever. Thus it was that Maung Hpay performed the great renunciation. From home he went forth to homelessness.

* * * *

Four years had passed away since Maung Hpay had entered the holy condition of monkhood. In a monastery at Moulmein he lived a life of strenuous self-discipline.

But what was it that Maung Hpay wanted? For what was he striving?

Maung Hpay wanted freedom from pain. He strove for freedom from sorrow. For, whosoever lays hold of the great thought of Transiency, for him life becomes sorrow. But he for whom all life has become sorrow, desires nothing, thinks of nothing but how to win to freedom from this sorrow. He alone, however, can be rid of this sorrow, who abandons, not only goods and gear, wife and child, but his own *I* also. He must abandon it; he must renounce it; he must deny it.

At this task Maung Hpay laboured day and night. But, as water always flows downwards, so his thoughts ever and again returned to wife and child and all that he had formerly called his own. Thus it was that he clung to this life. But to cling to this life is nothing but to cling to sorrow. Often and often he would have given up the struggle in despair, but something inside him cried, "Dig! dig! Whoso only digs deep enough will surely find the refreshing water."

One day, as he passed through the town upon his begging round, he came upon a great company of pilgrims, who had made their camp in the mango grove. It was, in fact, the month of Vessak, when Burma goes upon pilgrimage. The hill-pagoda of Moulmein is a sacred place, almost as sacred as the Golden Pagoda of Rangoon. The pilgrims come in large companies and camp out in the grove before they go up to worship, and each cooks his rice and curry near his cart.

Silently, with downcast eyes, Maung Hpay made his way from cart to cart, and everywhere rice was put into his bowl. As soon as he had received it he passed silently on, without a word of thanks and with eyes still lowered. It is in this fashion that the disciples of the Buddha beg for alms.

His bowl was about half full. He moved on to another cart.

"Mother, let me give the holy man something," he heard a childish voice say.

Involuntarily he glanced up beneath his lowered eyelids, for nature is stronger than art. Startled, he cast his eyes to the ground again. There before him stood his wife and Maung Tok. His wife was carrying a little baby in her arms. In front of both, however, stood a handsome, well-dressed boy of about six or seven years of age.

Once more Maung Hpay's eyes turned swiftly towards them. "My child!" his heart within him cried. He wanted to fling away the alms-bowl he held out and flee the place—or embrace his child?—he scarcely knew which. With a superhuman effort he mastered himself, but his hands trembled. None of them recognised him. For, this emaciated, aged-looking man with the bare skull, in the monk's yellow robe—what had he to do with that Maung Hpay before whom the people had been accustomed to bow and say, "How do you do, Maung Hpay?"

Meanwhile, his little son emptied ladleful after ladleful into his bowl. Then he added a lot of curry, so that the bowl was quite heaped up like a miniature tower.

"My child," Maung Hpay now heard his wife say softly, "in giving also, one must practise moderation."

The words expressed not greed, but simply carefulness. Maung Hpay understood.

"Never mind him, dear," said Maung Tok. "You know, we have so much to be thankful for. To whom can one show his thanks better than to this holy man?" He went over to the woman and petted the child that lay in her arms. "My sweet little daughter, my good wife," he said tenderly.

Meanwhile, the boy came running forward, and, throwing his arms round the man, said—

"Kiss me, too, father."

And Maung Tok kissed the boy, and stroked his hair.

Maung Hpay stood as if rooted to the ground. No one paid any attention to him. He had received gift and salutation, and with that all duty towards him as a monk had been discharged. The weight of his full alms-bowl brought him to himself. True to old habit, he put it under his outer garment and passed along the street. He walked on through all the carts out into the open, further and further, until he came to the hill in which are the caves used by the monks as places for meditation.

Into one of these Maung Hpay entered. He laid his bowl down at the entrance, and with crossed legs sat himself down in the gloom beyond. Clasping his hands tightly in one another, and firmly compressing his lips, he said to himself—

" The burden of this life I will not bear any longer. Here, in face of this full alms-bowl, I will starve till I die of hunger."

Then he drew within himself the life-essences, as he had learnt to do in the course of his ascetic exercises, and for hour after hour sat there motionless like some being void of life.

Day passed. The twilight of the cave changed to deepest darkness. Only the alms-bowl at the entrance stood out in relief against the softly illuminated background of the moonlit night outside. And now the death-like stillness of the woods began to be alive. The hoarse clamour of hyenas sounded quite close at hand; but Maung Hpay heard nothing. Now something stirred overhead in the foliage of the tree that stood in front of the cave. A hunted bird screeched out shrilly. Still Maung Hpay did not hear. Now the ground hummed, the twigs crackled. A herd of elephants drew slowly near to drink, and still Maung Hpay was deaf to everything. His half-shut eyes were glazed; no indrawn breath expanded his breast; and then—a soft rustling in the dry leaves that covered the floor of the cave. Then a sharp metallic hiss. Maung Hpay shrank up. It was the tone to which his ear was at present attuned. Life came into his eyes. He drew a deep breath. Now he heard the hissing. It was a snake. Now he saw it moving in the moonlit opening of the cave, there where his rice-filled bowl stood. Now it lifted itself up, and he recognised its thick head quite clearly against the illuminated background. It was a Tik Polonga, the most dangerous of poisonous snakes. Now the creature lowered its head and began, picking daintily, to devour the rice—the rice that Maung Hpay's little son had put into the bowl. But it soon left the bowl. For a moment it disappeared. Then Maung Hpay heard a rustling quite close to him. Now something cold slowly, slowly drew itself over his bare leg. He felt the horror of it running up his spine. He wanted to jump up and shake the creature off, but the slightest movement would have meant death, for the Tik Polonga is that snake which attacks. He felt as if he must cry out with terror, but he kept himself motionless. Now the creature must lay itself all its length in his lap—he felt its weight. And now—smooth and cold, its head was raised up, as if in search, to the level of his bare breast and yet higher. In frantic terror Maung Hpay turned the pupils of his eyes inwards till the muscles grated on one another, and dazzling sparks danced before him in the darkness. But he remained motionless, for movement would have been death. Still searching, the head again moved downwards. The creature again composed itself on his lap, part of its clammy length resting upon his clenched hands.

So for hour after hour did Maung Hpay sit motionless as the creature itself. But the height of horror, the extreme limit of possible emotion was past. His blood began to circulate more and more placidly, his distracted brain more and more to resume its normal activity. With eyes accustomed to the darkness of the cave he now recognised clearly the creature in his lap. It lay coiled up and evidently asleep. Maung Hpay looked at it for long. He wished to accustom himself to this sight, to conquer it, to make himself master of the situation. A smile passed over his features. "How foolish a creature is man!" he thought. "I sit myself down here, in order that of my own free will I may die a miserable death, then this creature comes along and, instead of giving it joyful welcome as a bringer of consolation, a saviour, every fibre of my *I* is seized with fright. It is all the fault of our ignorance. The outward appearance of things confuses us. We overcome this fear—that care; but, with each new day, a new fear, a new care arises that formerly was not there. How can man be at peace if he does not go to the root of all fear, if he does not annihilate the kernel of all anxiety? This *I* must be annihilated; we must abandon it, deny it, renounce it. This only can be called cutting off the root of all fear, trampling under foot the kernel of all anxiety; this alone is peace, safety, freedom."

Thereupon his mind was again caught in the great thought of transiency as the bolt is caught in the staple. He began to perceive more and more clearly the flux of all things, the merely seeming being of this entire world. But if the whole world is nothing but a beingless appearance, nothing but a delusion of the senses, then the idea of this *I* of mine is in itself really nothing but a delusion that deludes itself. Already for long Maung Hpay had been aware of this, but what he had hitherto only been aware of, as one is aware of the limbs of another person than one's self—this he now felt as one feels one's own limbs. In the glow of the hours that had just gone over his head the fruit of long years had come to ripeness. Maung Hpay smiled serenely. A blessed, hitherto unknown serenity filled him to overflowing. Again and again he indulged himself in the joy of the rising and falling of his thoughts. Again and again he indulged himself in the joy of this work of denial. For, is there a more joyful task than the denial, the renunciation of this wretched body, when once one has recognised its true nature, its painful nothingness? Is there any work more blissful than to assure one's self again and yet again, "For me this world is no more; all that was to do is done?" Suddenly a great weariness came over Maung Hpay, and, snake in lap, he fell into slumber. For, the man who has renounced his *I* may sleep well even with a snake in his lap.

Maung Hpay began to dream. He dreamt that he awoke. His first thought was, "Am I awake, or am I only dreaming?" He looked round the cave. "Here are the old withered leaves; there stands the alms-bowl, and here in my lap lies this snake." At the very moment, however, that he looked at the snake, the snake also looked at him. Slowly it lifted up its head. It seemed swollen. "How poisonous is this snake!" thought Maung Hpay. And now it was darting out its tongue right in his face. He looked serenely into the open jaws. "These teeth," he said to himself, "contain something that can destroy this my bodily form more speedily than I can say the words. But what does that signify? Is not Liberation also the losing of this form? Why get terrified at that? What is subject to death is already dead. How fortunate that I am awake to taste the blessedness of being set free!"

Quietly, kindly, he looked into the creature's flashing eyes. Then he perceived that it was not a snake at all, but his little son who was smiling at him. But Maung Hpay did not smile back. He thought, "This being that I have begotten has come from some quarter—I know not whence—and goes in some other direction—I know not whither." As he so thought, it lifted itself higher and higher. It expanded, it melted away. A misty light filled the cave, and suddenly the Tathāgata stood before him, lotus-throned, lineaments divine, garments glowing. From the lotus-throne downwards, however, all was enveloped in twilight.

Maung Hpay looked with unchanged

equanimity. "How strange," he thought, "that I am not astonished, that I am not rejoiced! But I have renounced this *I*—have denied it. At what shall I be astonished? At what rejoiced? There is none here to be astonished or rejoiced."

As he so reflected, the Tathāgata disappeared, and now he saw that the first beams of the rising sun were falling directly upon him through the opening of the cave. He looked into his lap,—it was empty. Maung Hpay thought for a moment, like one who tries to make sure whether he has only dreamt something or actually lived through it. With that, his eyes fell upon the alms-bowl. "What am I still sitting here for? I must rise and get ready for my begging-round." But sleep still lay on him. He jumped up nimbly, shook out his robe vigorously, and stepped towards his bowl with intent to pick it up. Then he saw that it was full of rice. He stopped short. Again he thought for a moment. Then he bent down to see, and smelt at the rice. It smelt badly. Then he knew that the snake had really devoured some of that child's rice, for whatever a snake eats at becomes evil-smelling almost immediately.

Yet once more he stood still in thought. Then he carefully emptied everything out upon a piece of ground free from grass, and, bowl on back, and eyes steadfastly fixed on the ground, went forth with firm steps towards the town to beg his daily food. For whoso has renounced his own *I*—he desires not death, he desires not life. He waits until the hour comes, patiently and with watchful mind. He waits until this mortal form of itself falls in ruins.

Thus it was that Maung Hpay completed his great renunciation.

THE END